PHARMACY TECHNICIAN MNEMONICS

A Memorizing Pharmacology Practice Exam Study Guide for the PTCB's PTCE and NHA's ExCPT Pharmacy Technician Exams

Tony Guerra, M.HCI., Pharm.D.

Pharmacy Technician Mnemonics: A Memorizing Pharmacology Study Guide for the PTCB's PTCE and NHA's ExCPT Pharmacy Technician Exams

Tony Guerra, M.HCI., Pharm.D.
First Edition
ISBN: 978-1-957259-02-4

To Mindy,
Brielle, Rianne, and Teagan

AUTHOR'S NOTE

MEMORIZING PRACTICE EXAMS

Wether you are taking the Pharmacy Technician Certification Exam (PTCE) which some call the PTCB which actually stands for the name of the organization, the Pharmacy Technician Certification Board, or the ExCPT, Exam for the Certification of Pharmacy Technicians administered by the National Healthcareer Association (NHA), there will be a point where you start taking a lot of practice exams. What I want to do with this book, that's a little different than the Memorizing Pharmacology parent book, is talk about how to memorize what you learned from taking and reviewing those exams so you can have all of those questions and answers in your long-term memory as you enter the ultimate licensing exam.

In *Memorizing Pharmacology: A Relaxed Approach*, I introduced the acronym GMRINCE, where you start by memorizing the seven pathophysiologic classes in the book in order as G-M-RINCE, as Grand Mothers RINCE kids' hair (except it's the French r-i-n-c-e instead of the English r-i-n-s-e) to set up the broadest framework. These seven pathophysiologic classes help as steel reinforcing bars that, when surrounded by concrete, will provide the foundation for your memorizing the gastrointestinal (G), musculoskeletal (M), respiratory (R), immune (I), neuro (N), cardio (C), and endocrine (E) systems' medications.

AUTHOR'S NOTE

Students would take the mnemonic and put it on a notecard for later practice. For the licensing exam, we are going to create a way to sort our 3 x 5 notecards into twelve distinct piles, rather than seven. Personally, I would do this all in twelve tabs of an Excel spreadsheet, but do what works for you.

I will now add five more letters to make a 12-letter acronym for pharmacy technicians, "GM RINCED ALSO," G-M-R-I-N-C-E-D-A-L-S-O. for

G – gastrointestinal

M – musculoskeletal

R – respiratory

I – Immune and Integumentary (skin)

N – Neuro/Psych

C – Cardio

E – Endocrine, Etc

D – Dosage Calculations

A – Abbreviations, Acronyms, and Initialisms

L – Laws and Regulations

S – Supplements

O – Other Questions

As you take the practice exams, what you want to do is recognize where in your brain you stored the information.

To do that, you have to create specific containers for that knowledge. Just as you would look for a coffee cup in the kitchen of your house or a pillow in the bedroom, you would look for the -prazole, p-r-a-z-o-l-e suffix in, G, gastrointestinal and the -dronate, d-r-o-n-a-t-e suffix in M, musculoskeletal, and 2.2 pounds = 1 kilogram in D, dosage calculations.

Let me show you how this works with a practice question.

A patient brings a bottle of echinacea to the pharmacy counter, what condition are they trying to treat?

    A. Depression
    B. Insomnia
    C. Cold symptoms
    D. BPH

We're going to take a quick trip to the S – Supplements pile of notecards or spreadsheet tab and look at all the questions we've answered before on that topic.

With supplements, especially herbals, there's usually one really specific condition that matches up with it. So, what you should see after you finish this book, just as a practicing professional would, is:

    A. Depression – St. John's Wort
    B. Insomnia – Valerian Root
    C. Cold symptoms – Echinacea
    D. BPH – Saw Palmetto

Makes it a heck of a lot easier to answer the question, right?

AUTHOR'S NOTE

What I'm going to do with this book, which is quite different than regular practice exams you'll find in other books, is go through them in order. Let me tell you why.

AN ORDERED PRACTICE EXAM TO START

If you are a major league batter, you need to be able to hit many different types of pitches. In the very instant that pitch leave's the pitcher's hand, the batter must quickly assess whether they are going to swing at a fastball, slider, sinker, curveball, change-up and so on. A practice exam is just like batting 90 or 100 times. Each pitch will likely be different than the last and even the same pitch can have a different placement.

However, if you want to get good at hitting a *specific pitch*, you wouldn't keep trying to hit all the different pitches. You would buckle down and work on hitting against the curve in one practice session and the slider in another. The skills you use are different. In the same way, I'm going to present the practice exam questions in order. You'll have a chapter to practice against GI fast balls, musculoskeletal curves, and respiratory sliders and so on so you can keep remembering what you learn.

From then on, you'll always be able to "code" each practice exam question as one of the 12 I've outlined. Some students go so far as to make each category its own color. For example, green for GI (I'm feeling green), blue for not breathing, and red for cardiac and heart make a lot of sense to me.

WHY ONLY 12 DIVISIONS?

I understand there are many more divisions that we can use, different types of dosage calculations, separating safety and other questions and so on. But what I've done is taken the most recognizable questions as a way to speed this process. There is no doubt when you see a dosage calculations question, a law question, or one dealing with a certain aspect of pharmacology.

The way I ordered these is that if there are multiple drug classes in the question or answer, it is the drug class of the correct answer that I put as the ultimate class. For example, if the question reads:

An antifungal that can help a patient with with a yeast infection would most likely be:

    A. fluoxetine
    B. fluconazole
    C. omeprazole
    D. esomeprazole

I would classify this question as Room 4, I, immune and integumentary question, and place that answer in my Excel spreadsheet or 3 x 5 notecard pile. When I approach this question, as you will learn in the book, you will also see the answer choices much more completely as:

    A. fluoxetine (Prozac, Serafem) antidepressant
    B. fluconazole (Diflucan) antifungal
    C. omeprazole – (Prilosec) PPI
    D. aripiprazole – (Abilify) Antipsychotic

FINAL NOTE

If you pass your certification exam, feel free to email me:

tonythepharmacist@gmail.com

I want to share in your victory and I'm always looking for better ways to teach pharm. If you see a student struggling with the language of pharmacology who doesn't have this book or a patient who wants to better understand his or her many prescriptions, please do take the time to recommend it to them.

There was a pharmacology class that I got a standing ovation, just like in the 1972 movie *The Paper Chase*. I hope what you get out of this book is worth your standing up.

Table of Contents

Contents

Contents

Contents

INTRODUCTION

A Practice Exam Walkthrough

When I coached cross-country runners, we would always walk through the course before the race. We would look for opportunities to catch a little more speed, pitfalls to avoid, and put these to memory in the order of the course. In the same way, I'm going to walk through a full exam with you giving you the inner thoughts I have a as a professor. You'll see how looking at each question as a puzzle rather than a peril will make it a lot more fun and easier to not only prepare for the exam, but ultimately pass it.

We're going to go by body system and each 10th question is a dosing calculations question within that body system. So, question G1 stands for gastrointestinal question 1, but question GD10 is gastrointestinal dosage calculations question 10.

When I see something complex with a lot to memorize, I'll add a mnemonic to help you remember the drugs that are in each DEA Drug Schedule, ones we have to worry about sunlight, or those that need to be taken with water and so on.

Let's get started!

PRACTICE EXAM PART 1 GASTROINTESTINAL

QUESTION G1.

Which of the following is an H-2 antagonist for heartburn?

a) Esomeprazole
b) Bismuth subsalicylate
c) Calcium carbonate
d) Famotidine

ANSWER.

Which of the following is an H-2 antagonist for heartburn?

a) Esomeprazole
b) Bismuth subsalicylate
c) Calcium carbonate
d) Famotidine

Answer: D. Famotidine. The first thing I do when I see a list of medications is write down or mentally go through all of the suffixes, brand names, and therapeutic uses.

A. Esomeprazole (Nexium), prazole, p-r-a-z-o-l-e suffix proton pump inhibitor (PPI) for GERD.

B. Bismuth subsalicylate, (Pepto Bismol) for Diarrhea/upset stomach with the sal, s-a-l salicylate stem.

C. Calcium carbonate (Tums, Children's Pepto), an Antacid that has not suffix, but the brand Tums helps me know it's for someone's tummy.

D. Famotidine (Pepcid), with the H-2 Blocker tidine, t-i-d-i-n-e suffix for GERD which makes this the correct answer.

QUESTION G2.

A patient has severe diarrhea and needs diphenoxylate with atropine (Lomotil), what DEA Schedule would this fall under.

    a) II
    b) III
    c) IV
    d) V

ANSWER.

A patient has severe diarrhea and needs diphenoxylate with atropine (Lomotil), what DEA Schedule would this fall under.

a) II
b) III
c) IV
d) V

Answer: D, V. I created a mnemonic to remember the common medications in a drug class. Remember, a single letter I is a 1, two IIs are 2, three II's are three, IV is four, which looks just like IV for intravenous and a letter V alone is five. The DEA C-V mnemonic sounds like this.

MNEMONIC – C-V DRUGS – FIVE PACED

P	Pregabalin (Lyrica)
A/C	And Cough as in Robitussin AC or Cheratussin AC
E	Elixers 200 mg of codeine in every 100 mL
D	Diphenoxylate/Atropine

You can also use mnemonics for the other four DEA classes.

MNEMONIC – C-I DRUGS – ONE HELM

With this one, think you have one head, so one helm for the C-I medications.

H	Heroin
E	Ecstacy

L	LSD
M	Marijuana

Mnemonic – C-II Drugs – TWO CHAMP FOG

With this one think of a two-time boxing champ in a fog with the medications in the DEA Schedule II.

C	Cocaine
H	Hydrocodone/hydromorphone
A	Amphetamine/amobarbital
M	Methamphetamine/methadone, methylphenidate
P	Pentobarbital
F	Fentanyl
O	Oxycodone
G	Glutethimide

Mnemonic – C-III Drugs – THREE TACKS TEST

If you imagine a test that you got an A on with three tacks in the corkboard, you can remember testosterone and the other medications in the C-III DEA Drug Schedule.

T	Testosterone
A/C	Acetaminophen/Codeine 90 milligrams or less per dosage unit
K	Ketamine
S	Steroids, anabolic

MNEMONIC – C-IV DRUGS – FOUR CALM CATTTZ

Think of four cats sleeping, but just spelled differently for the DEA Schedule C-IV medications.

C	Clonazepam (Klonopin)
A	Alprazolam (Xanax)
L	Lorazepam (Ativan)
M	Midazolam (Versed)
C	Carisoprodol (Soma)
A	Ambien (brand name of zolpidem)
T	Tramadol (Ultram)
T	Temazepam (Restoril)
T	Triazolam (Halcion)
Z	Zaleplon (Sonata)

QUESTION G3.

You read the following prescription:

Omeprazole 20 mg ODT Sig: Give 1 tab daily for reflux #30
Refills = 2

What is the means of administration?

a) Intranasally
b) Subcutaneously
c) **On the tongue**
d) In the cheek

ANSWER.

You read the following prescription:

Omeprazole 20 mg ODT Sig: Give 1 tab daily for reflux #30
Refills = 2

What is the means of administration?

a) Intranasally
b) Subcutaneously
c) On the tongue
d) In the cheek

Answer: C, On the tongue. ODT stands for orally
disintegrating tablets and there are many meds that come
ODT, but not all use those letters. Here are some examples
in the FOLD, creates an ODD CALM mnemonic as these
ODTs calm patients who don't want to swallow tablets.

MNEMONIC – ODT– FOLD CREATES ODD CALM

F	Fexofenadine (Allegra ODT)
O	Ondansetron (Zofran ODT)
L	Lamotrigine (Lamictal ODT)
D	Donepezil (Aricept ODT)

O	Olanzapine (Zyprexa Zydis)
D	Desloratadine (Claritin RediTabs)
D	Diphenhydramine (Benadryl FastMelt)

C	Cetirizine (Zyrtec Dissolve Tabs)
A	Acetaminophen (Jr. Tylenol Meltaways)
L	Loratadine (Clarinex RediTabs)
M	Mirtazapine (Remeron SolTab)

QUESTION G4.

A prescriber prescribes nizatidine for which condition?

a) Jock itch
b) Asthma
c) Heartburn
d) Respiratory infection

ANSWER.

A prescriber prescribes nizatidine for which condition?

  a) Jock itch
  b) Asthma
  c) Heartburn
  d) Respiratory infection

Answer: C, Heartburn. What you can do with this list is write your anticipated suffixes, so it reads:

A. Jock itch: -conazole

B. Asthma: -terol, -sone, -lukast, -tropium

C. Heartburn: -prazole, -tidine which is at the end of nizatidine.

D. Respiratory infection: -floxacin, -cillin, -thromycin

Then when we return to the question, we see that nizatidine has one of those endings, the -tidine, t-i-d-i-n-e from an H-2 blocker for GERD and heartburn. Another way to approach it, is to ensure that you know the nizatidine brand name Axid, A-x-i-d, which is one letter from Acid, a-c-i-d so you know the medicine is for excess acid, a cause of heartburn.

QUESTION G5.

You would expect which interaction between the following over-the-counter and prescription medication?

Calcium carbonate (Tums)

Ciprofloxacin (Cipro)

a) Chelation
b) Bleeding
c) Diarrhea
d) GI upset

ANSWER.

You would expect which interaction between the following over-the-counter and prescription medication?

Calcium carbonate (Tums)

Ciprofloxacin (Cipro)

a) Chelation
b) Bleeding
c) Diarrhea
d) GI upset

Answer: A, Chelation. There are some interactions that are must-know interactions or side effects from medications. Immediately, your brain should associate these common side effects with certain drugs and/or drug classes so it actually looks like this:

MNEMONIC – CHELATING WITH DRUGS - ATOMIC

A	Aluminum
T	Tetracycline
O	Ofloxacin
M	Magnesium
I	Iron
C	Calcium

So, in this case, the chelation is the issue between a drug with the -floxacin stem and calcium carbonate, but it could have just as easily been a drug-food interaction with ciprofloxacin and milk or drug-supplement interaction between ciprofloxacin and iron.

QUESTION G6.

Which medication is most appropriate for a patient with diarrhea?

a) Prilosec
b) Milk-of-Magnesia
c) Pepcid
d) Imodium

Answer: D, Imodium. With all brand names, we want more information, so we would expand all of these either on paper or mentally to read like this:

A. Prilosec – omeprazole, PPI for GERD

B. Milk-of-Magnesia, magnesium hydroxide, antacid

C. Pepcid – famotidine, H-2 blocker

D. Imodium – loperamide, antidiarrheal

Chapter 1 Gastrointestinal

ANSWER.

Which medication is most appropriate for a patient with diarrhea?

a) Prilosec
b) Milk-of-Magnesia
c) Pepcid
d) Imodium

Answer: D, Imodium. With all brand names, we want more information, so we would expand all of these either on paper or mentally to read like this:

A. Prilosec – omeprazole, PPI for GERD

B. Milk-of-Magnesia, magnesium hydroxide, antacid

C. Pepcid – famotidine, H-2 blocker

D. Imodium – loperamide, antidiarrheal

This is a tricky question because all of the answers have to do with gastrointestinal conditions, but the first three are really acid reducers of some sort or another which don't really help a patient with diarrhea. Worse, magnesium hydroxide has diarrhea as a side effect.

The mnemonic from Memorizing Pharmacology for generic loperamide is to see "low peristalsis" or low intestinal movement and to recognize part of the work "immobile" in the Imodium brand name that can also help you get to the right answer quickly.

QUESTION G7.

The following electronic prescription comes to the pharmacy:

Promethazine 25 mg #12

Sig: Use 1 supp PR as directed 4 times daily.

What is the method of administration?

a) Rectal
b) Oral
c) Subcutaneously
d) Intramuscularly

ANSWER.

The following electronic prescription comes to the pharmacy:

Promethazine 25 mg #12

Sig: Use 1 supp PR as directed 4 times daily.

What is the method of administration?

a) **Rectal**
b) Oral
c) Subcutaneously
d) Intramuscularly

Answer: A, Rectal. First, I think of the abbreviations for these answers.

A. Rectal – PR, per rectum

B. Oral – PO, per os, by mouth (literally per opening)

C Subcut – One safety question you will often get is the correct way to safely write this and it is to write "subcut" or "subcutaneously" rather than SC, SQ or sub q.

D. Intramuscularly – IM

Sometimes you can get the answer without knowing the Latin abbreviation at all. Promethazine comes as aa suppository and suppositories are administered vaginally or rectally, and only one of those is an option. Also, promethazine has two distinct uses, one as a preventative for nausea and another as an antihistamine in cough medicine. By considering the product package and its therapeutic use, you can answer the question.

QUESTION G8.

Which of the following auxiliary labels should be on a docusate prescription?

a) Take with water
b) Use sunscreen
c) Take at bedtime
d) Shake well

ANSWER.

Which of the following auxiliary labels should be on a docusate prescription?

a) **Take with water**
b) Use sunscreen
c) Take at bedtime
d) Shake well

Answer: A, Take with water. Docusate is a pill, so we would immediately remove "Shake Well." We then see docusate on this list to take with water.

MNEMONIC - TAKE WITH WATER - FLUIDS

F	Furosemide
L	aLlopurinol
U	UTI, Phenazopyridine and SMZ/TMP
I	Ibandronate
D	Docusate
S	Sulfa Antibiotics

And we don't see it on this use sunscreen list.

MNEMONIC - USE SUNCREEN – HOT SUN CAN (BURN)

H	Hydrochlorothiazide (Microzide)
O	Ofloxacin (Floxin)
T	Tetracycline (Sumycin)
SU	SUlfamethoxazole/trimethoprim (Bactrim)
N	Naproxen (Aleve) (NSAIDS in general)
C	Ciprofloxacin (Cipro) (Quinolones in general)
A	Amiodarone (Cordarone)
N	Nortriptyline (Pamelor) (TCAs, in general)

QUESTION G9.

In deprescribing medications, a prescriber will remove a medication used for prophylaxis that is no longer necessary. Which of the following medications could represent a proton pump inhibitor that is no longer needed by a patient for prophylaxis?

a) Colace
b) Nexium
c) Tums
d) MiraLax

ANSWER.

In deprescribing medications, a prescriber will remove a medication used for prophylaxis that is no longer necessary. Which of the following medications could represent a proton pump inhibitor that is no longer needed by a patient for prophylaxis?

a) Colace
b) Nexium
c) Tums
d) MiraLax

Answer: B, Nexium. In some questions, it's possible to hide the answer by using the brand names. So, mentally, or in writing, it's ideal to again translate these medications to their generic names, stems, and drug classes.

A. Colace, docusate sodium, surfactant laxative/stool softener

B. Nexium, esomeprazole, -prazole, proton pump inhibitor

C. Tums, calcium carbonate, antacid

D. MiraLax, polyethylene glycol, osmotic laxative

One you complete the answer expansion, the answer becomes clear – Nexium. Even if you didn't remember this exactly, you could use that Nexium was the next proton pump inhibitor after Prilosec, omeprazole, or that the "p-r" in prazole can stand for protons.

QUESTION GD10.

A patient is to take bismuth subsalicylate liquid 2 tbsp PO q 1 hr for no greater than 8 doses in a day. What then, is the maximum daily dose in mL?

a) 60 mL
b) 120 mL
c) 240 mL
d) 300 mL

ANSWER.

A patient is to take bismuth subsalicylate liquid 2 tbsp PO q 1 hr for no greater than 8 doses in a day. What then, is the maximum daily dose in mL?

a) 60 mL
b) 120 mL
c) **240 mL**
d) 300 mL

Answer: C, 240 mL/ day.

While I understand calculations are a real concern for most that take the exam, the most important thing to do is get a confident first step. Most calculations problems will have the units in the multiple-choice answer and except for alligations, can be solved by dimensional analysis, also known as the factor label method.

So, your first step should be to set up the fence or table and put in the label as the answer.

			mL
			day

You want to memorize the process, then work on memorizing individual problems. I actually do math backwards from right to left because I follow the clues, but most of my students prefer to go from left to right. However, the right to left method is a great tool to have if you get stuck. One thing that will help you a lot is to take the 30 seconds to write out the factors as you will not always use all of them.

Pharmacy Tech Mnemonics

Factors:

| 1 tbsp / 15 mL | 8 doses / 1 day | 1 dose / 2 tbsp |

Then put in the factors

8 **doses**	2 tbsp	15 mL	mL
1 day	1 **dose**	1 tbsp	day

Then solve

8 ~~doses~~	2 ~~tbsp~~	15 mL	240 mL
1 day	1 ~~dose~~	1 ~~tbsp~~	day

PRACTICE EXAM PART 2
MUSCULOSKELETAL

QUESTION M11.

Your patient always comes to ask about OTC medications because they are on warfarin, and they know there are many interactions. Which analgesic is ideal for this patient?

    a) Aleve
    b) Motrin
    c) Advil
    d) Tylenol

ANSWER.

Your patient always comes to ask about OTC medications because they are on warfarin, and they know there are many interactions. Which analgesic is ideal for this patient?

a) Aleve
b) Motrin
c) Advil
d) Tylenol

Answer:D, Tylenol. With all brand names, we want more information, so we would expand all of these either on paper or mentally making the answer apparent. NSAIDs can cause bleeding and ulceration, however, acetaminophen, unlike the NSAIDs does not cause this effect.

A. Aleve, naproxen, NSAID

B. Motrin, ibuprofen, NSAID

C. Advil, ibuprofen, NSAID

D. Tylenol, acetaminophen, a non-narcotic analgesic

QUESTION M12.

There is a mistake in the following prescription, please identify it.

Sumatriptan injection 6 mg/0.5 mL (Imitrex)
Inject one dose IM at onset of migraine

An error appears to have been made in the medication's:

    a) Generic name
    b) Direction
    c) Administration route
    d) Strength

ANSWER.

There is a mistake in the following prescription, please identify it.

Sumatriptan injection 6 mg/0.5 mL (Imitrex)
Inject one dose IM at onset of migraine

An error appears to have been made in the medication's:

a) Generic name
b) Direction
c) Administration route
d) Strength

Answer: C, Administration route. Finding a mistake or even what is not there is difficult as a true error happens so rarely. We can see that the generic name and brand name match.

A. Sumatriptan, and triptans in general, trip up headaches.

B. The direction does not indicate what to do if a second dose is needed, but the current direction is not wrong.

C. The difficulty with this question comes from never having actually seeing a patient use a sumatriptan injection. With an influenza vaccine, a patient may have seen that the needle goes in at 90 degrees for an intramuscular, IM, shot. With insulin, the dose is subcut, or at about 45 degrees under the skin in one inch can be pinched, or 90 degrees for two inches. This is unfortunately one of those many facts that should be memorized. You might use the first letter in sumatriptan to think S, subcutaneous for S, sumatriptan.

D. The strength is consistent with a sumatriptan injection.

QUESTION M13.

A prescriber provides a patient with a Vicoprofen prescription and patient asks if they can pay for their Benadryl and Advil in the same transaction. In your role, you should:

a) Ring up the transaction without comment
b) Let the patient know that the medicine in Vicoprofen and Advil are the same and they do not need to purchase Advil
c) Let the patient know the combination of Vicoprofen and Benadryl will cause extreme drowsiness and to wait until they drive home to use either
d) Ask the pharmacist to speak with the patient privately detailing your concerns to the pharmacist about the Advil and Benadryl

ANSWER.

A prescriber provides a patient with a Vicoprofen prescription and patient asks if they can pay for their Benadryl and Advil in the same transaction. In your role, you should:

    a) Ring up the transaction without comment
    b) Let the patient know that the medicine in Vicoprofen and Advil are the same and they do not need to purchase Advil
    c) Let the patient know the combination of Vicoprofen and Benadryl will cause extreme drowsiness and to wait until they drive home to use either
    d) Ask the pharmacist to speak with the patient privately detailing your concerns to the pharmacist about the Advil and Benadryl

Answer: D. Ask the pharmacist to speak with the patient privately detailing your concerns to the pharmacist about the Advil and Benadryl.

A. You don't want to ignore the concerns you have, so it's important to talk to the pharmacist.

B. Although Vicoprofen and Advil both contain ibuprofen, the technician may not provide this advice.

C. It is true an opioid like Vicoprofen and diphenhydramine, a first-generation antihistamine, will both cause drowsiness. However, it is up to the pharmacist to convey this information.

D. The pharmacist will convey the information as the technician ensures the pharmacist is aware of the dangers.

QUESTION M14.

A patient has a recent diagnosis of rheumatoid arthritis, and the prescriber is interested in slowing the progression of the disease. Which of the following is a biologic DMARD that the prescriber might ues to this end?

    a) Etanercept
    b) Ibuprofen
    c) Methotrexate
    d) Celecoxib

ANSWER.

A patient has a recent diagnosis of rheumatoid arthritis, and the prescriber is interested in slowing the progression of the disease. Which of the following is a biologic DMARD that the prescriber might ues to this end?

     a) Etanercept
     b) Ibuprofen
     c) Methotrexate
     d) Celecoxib

Answer: A, etanercept (Enbrel). This question benefits from expanding the generic names to generic name and drug class.to make the answer readily apparent.

A. Etanercept (Enbrel), Biologic DMARD for RA

B. Ibuprofen, (Advil, Motrin), NSAID for arthritis

C. Methotrexate (Rheumatrex), Non-biologic DMARD for RA

D. Celecoxib (Celebrex), Second-generation NSAID for arthritis.

Sometimes you may know what the other three medications are and deduce that A is the answer if if you'd never seen that question.

QUESTION M15.

Which medication is most appropriate for a patient with osteoporosis, weak and brittle bones?

a) Ibandronate
b) Sumatriptan
c) Meloxicam
d) Etanercept

ANSWER.

Which medication is most appropriate for a patient with osteoporosis, weak and brittle bones?

 a) **Ibandronate**
 b) Sumatriptan
 c) Meloxicam
 d) Etanercept

Answer: A. Ibandronate. Again, opening up the answer choices with brand names, stems and drug classes is key.

A. Iban<u>dronate</u>, (Boniva), osteoporosis

B. Suma<u>triptan</u>, (Imitrex), migraines

C. Melox<u>icam</u> (Mobic), NSAID

D. Eta<u>nercept</u>, (Enbrel), DMARD

QUESTION M16.

A high alert medication class would most likely include:

a) NSAIDs
b) Sulfonylureas
c) Non-narcotic analgesics
d) Triptans

ANSWER.

A high alert medication class would most likely include:

    a) NSAIDs
    b) Sulfonylureas
    c) Non-narcotic analgesics
    d) Triptans

Answer: B. Sulfonylureas. Here is where we can get into the weeds with memorization. When you see "high alert," ask yourself which is the most dangerous medication class? In the case of sulfonylureas, we might see very quick hypoglycemia, but all of these drug classes are dangerous in one way or another. The "endoplasmic" is from endoplasmic reticulum back in biology, the eukaroyotic cell's transport system.

MNEMONIC – HIGH ALERT MEDICATION CLASSES - ENDOPLASMIC

E	Epidurals
N	Neuromuscular blockers (NMBs)
D	Dialysis solutions
O	Opioids
P	Parenteral nutrition
L	Liposomals like amphotericin B
A	Antiarrythmics and antithrombotics
S	Sulfonylureas
M	Moderate / Minimal sedation in IV Pediatrics
I	Insulin
C	Chemotherapy

QUESTION M17.

A Duragesic prescription comes to the pharmacy with a DAW 1 code. The patient would like to use fentanyl, a much less expensive generic. What is the issue?

a) By writing Duragesic, rather than fentanyl, the prescriber has not allowed the pharmacy to dispense anything other than Duragesic
b) There is no issue, the patient can get the fentanyl generic product
c) The pharmacist will need to decide if the patient can have the generic
d) The pharmacist will simply need to provide counseling as if the fentanyl is a new prescription

ANSWER.

A Duragesic prescription comes to the pharmacy with a DAW 1 code. The patient would like to use fentanyl, a much less expensive generic. What is the issue?

a) **By writing Duragesic, rather than fentanyl, the prescriber has not allowed the pharmacy to dispense anything other than Duragesic**
b) There is no issue, the patient can get the fentanyl generic product
c) The pharmacist will need to decide if the patient can have the generic
d) The pharmacist will simply need to provide counseling as if the fentanyl is a new prescription

Answer: A. By writing Duragesic, rather than fentanyl, the prescriber mandates Duragesic. There are 10 DAW codes from 0 to 9, here's a way to remember them, but when you think about how often the DAWs are used, it makes sense to put the most used DAW as 0, then the next most used DAW as 1 and so on. You want to group them in this way.

MNEMONIC – DAW CODES – 0, 178, 2345, 69

DAW 0	No product selection indicated
DAW 1 DAW 7 DAW 8	Substitution Not Allowed
DAW 2 DAW 3 DAW 4 DAW 5	Substitution Allowed
DAW 6 DAW 9	Undefined, not in general use.

Here's an expanded explanation with some mnemonics.

DAW 0 – No product selection

If you've ever been around a child who could care less what you have for dinner, that's DAW 0, no product selection, zero product selection

DAWs 1, 7, 8 – The three "Substition not allowed"

DAW 1 prescriber, DAW 7 law, or DAW 8 marketplace.

You can add 1 + 7 = 8 to keep these connected in your brain.

DAW 1 – Substitution not allowed by prescriber

DAW 7 – Substition not allowed as brand drug is mandated by law/regulation

DAW 8 – Substition not allowed as generic drug is not available in marketplace

DAWs 2, 3, 4, 5 Substitution allowed, patient, pharmacy, generic not in stock, brand as generic.

If you've every played Yahtzee or Poker, a 2,3,4,5 is a small straight to keep these DAWs together in your brain.

DAW 2 – Substitution allowed – patient requested product

DAW 3 – Substitution allowed – pharmacy requested drug

DAW 4 – Substitution allowed – generic drug not in stock

DAW 5 – Substitution allowed - Brand dispensed as generic

DAWs - 6,9 Undefined, not in general use; reserved for future use.

When you roll a nine or a six on any dice that have 10 or greater sides, you have to put an underline, so you know which way is up. That's how I remember 6 and 9 are undefined. Also, nine and undefined kind of rhyme.

QUESTION M18.

Identify the medication duo that would be a look-alike/sound-alike pairing as listed on the Food and Drug Administration-Approved List of Generic Drug Names with Tall Man Letters:

   a) Methotrexate and methylprednisolone
   b) Ibuprofen and naproxen
   c) Hydromorphone and hydroxyzine
   d) Sumatriptan and Suboxone

ANSWER.

Identify the medication duo that would be a look-alike/sound-alike pairing as listed on the Food and Drug Administration-Approved List of Generic Drug Names with Tall Man Letters:

  a) Methotrexate and methylprednisolone
  b) Ibuprofen and naproxen
  c) Hydromorphone and hydroxyzine
  d) Sumatriptan and Suboxone

Answer: C. Hydromorphone and hydroxyzine. When you think about look-alike/sound alike, try to find the pair that has both the beginning and end the same.

A. Methotrexate and methylprednisolone only look the same in the beginning, but only four letters in common at the beginning or end.

B. Ibuprofen and naproxen both end in -en, e-n, but only two letters in common at the beginning or end.

C. Hydromorphone and hydroxyzine both start with hydro and end with en, e-n, so that's seven letters in common.

D. Sumatriptan and suboxone – only two letters are the same in the beginning.

Why does this matter so much? Just as your brain fills in the blind spot where your optic nerve connects to your retina, your brain can read words even if the middle of the word is spelled incorrectly and make sense of it. So, your brain might confuse two drugs trying to rearrange the letters to something it recognizes.

QUESTION M19.

Generally, patients will take which medication just once weekly?

a) Alendronate
b) Oxycodone
c) Hydrocodone/acetaminophen
d) Acetaminophen/codeine

ANSWER.

Generally, patients will take which medication just once weekly?

a) **Alendronate**
b) Oxycodone
c) Hydrocodone/acetaminophen
d) Acetaminophen/codeine

Answer: A. Methotrexate. While we don't have to know exactly how often a patient takes every single medicine, there are some very notable exceptions for once weekly dosing. We can use the mnemonic methotrexate weekly adverbs, because the word weekly can be an adverb.

MNEMONIC – METHOTREXATE WEEKLY ADVERBS

M	Methotrexate
W	Weekly blockers
A	Alendronate (Fosamax)
D	Dulaglutide (Trulicity)
V	Vaginal Rings Three Weeks
E	Exenatide (Bydureon)
R	Risedronate (Actonel)
B	Birth Control Patches
S	Semaglutide (Ozempic)

QUESTION MD20.

A child needs 7.5 mL of ibuprofen over-the-counter liquid for pain every 6 hours around the clock. Each dose would then require how many tsp?

a) 1
b) 1.5
c) 2
d) 2.5

ANSWER.

A child needs 7.5 mL of ibuprofen over-the-counter liquid for pain every 6 hours around the clock. Each dose would then require how many tsp?

       a) 1
       b) 1.5
       c) 2
       d) 2.5

Answer: B. 1.5 tsp.

So, your first step should be to set up the fence or table and put in the label as the answer.

			tsp
			dose

Write out the factors as you will not always use all of them.

Conversion Factors:

1 dose / 7.5 mL

1 tsp / 5 mL

7.5 mL	1 tsp	tsp
1 dose	5 mL	dose

Then solve

7.5 ~~mL~~	1 tsp	1 ½ tsp
1 dose	5 ~~mL~~	dose

PRACTICE EXAM PART 3 RESPIRATORY

QUESTION R21.

Which is a look-alike/sound-alike pair?

a) Albuterol and salmeterol
b) Flovent and Atrovent
c) Ipratropium and tiotropium
d) Zyrtec and Zyprexa

Chapter 3 Respiratory

ANSWER.

Which is a look-alike/sound-alike pair?

    a) Albuterol and salmeterol
    b) Flovent and Atrovent
    c) Ipratropium and tiotropium
    d) Zyrtec and Zyprexa

Answer: D. Zyrtec and Zyprexa. When you look at these, it's important to know the difference between generic drug stems and brand name similarities and even on the most basic level, what makes a look-alike/sound-alike pair. It's somewhat subjective.

A. Albu<u>terol</u> and salme<u>terol</u> share the -terol, -t-e-r-o-l brochondilator, more specifically, beta-2 agonist stem.

B. Flovent and Atrovent are both brand names share the "vent, v-e-n-t"that speaks to their ability to improve ventilation for an asthmatic. Proventil and Ventolin are other brand name examples. With Flovent, we are contrasting a dosage form that is for asthma and inhaled versus Flonase which is for the nose.

C. Ipra<u>tropium</u> and Tio<u>tropium</u> share the -tropium, t-r-o-p-i-u-m stems indicating an anticholinergic, in this case for asthma or COPD.

D. Zyrtec and Zyprexa are very different. One is an antihistamine, and one is an antipsychotic. When you look at the sound-alike aspect, when you pronounce the letter "x" in Zyprexa, it is just like a hard c in Zyrtec. Combined with the Zy, Z-y, you get a look-alike/sound alike drug and is the correct answer.

QUESTION R22.

Which medicine would likely have anticholinergic effects?

   a) ProAir HFA
   b) DuoNeb
   c) Claritin
   d) Sudafed

ANSWER.

Which medicine would likely have anticholinergic effects?

a) ProAir HFA
b) DuoNeb
c) Claritin
d) Sudafed

Answer: B. DuoNeb. Expanding these brand names to discover their generic names will reveal the type of medications they are.

A. ProAir HFA, albuterol, with the -terol, t-e-r-o-l stem, is a beta-2 adrenergic medication, so not cholinergic.

B. DuoNeb is a duo of nebulization medications, albuterol, again with the terol, t-e-r-o-l stem, an adrenergic, but also ipratropium, with the tropium stem, an anticholinergic medication, so this is the correct answer. Again, cholinergic has to do with activating acetylcholine.

C. Claritin, loratadine, with the -atadine, a-t-a-d-i-n-e stem is a 2nd generation antihistamine with minimal drowsiness.

D. Sudafed, pseudoephedrine, with the -drine, -d-r-i-n-e suffix, is a sypathomimetic, that combines the word sympathetic and mime, that is mimicking the sympathetic system. It is an alpha adrenergic, so not cholinergic.

QUESTION R23.

An asthmatic is having frequent bouts of difficulty breathing and needs to try a prophylactic medication. Which medicine is most appropriate for a patient who needs an inhaled steroid?

a) Flonase
b) Advair
c) Singulair
d) Medrol

ANSWER.

An asthmatic is having frequent bouts of difficulty breathing and needs to try a prophylactic medication. Which medicine is most appropriate for a patient who needs an inhaled steroid?

a) Flonase
b) Advair
c) Singulair
d) Medrol

Answer: B. Advair. Again, we have to expand these brand names to see what's underneath.

A. Flonase's generic is fluticasone with the sone, s-o-n-e suffix. Although not an official suffix, this -sone indicates a steroid. However, the question asks for an inhaled steroid. Flovent HFA, would have been correct, but Flonase is for the nose and not an inhaled steroid for asthma.

B. Advair does "add air" to an asthmatic, but it also adds two medicines: salmeterol, with the terol, t-e-r-o-l stem, an adrenergic bronchodilator. But there is also fluticasone, with the -sone, s-o-n-e suffix, an inhaled steroid making this the correct answer. By the way, Advair comes in a package and once it's out of that packaging, it's good for a month.

C. Singulair, generic montelukast, is a leukotriene receptor antagonist. We can see many letters of leukotriene in montelukast and the once daily single dosing in Singulair.

D. Medrol, methylprednisolone, is also a steroid, we see the lone, l-o-n-e suffix which is unofficial, but is at the end of many steroids. However, methylprednisolone has oral and IV forms, but not an inhaled form to get right to the lungs without affecting the rest of the body as much.

QUESTION R24.

A patient comes to the pharmacy counter with the following over-the-counter medicine and tells you they run a lawn care business and spend quite a bit of the day driving. Which medicine would cause you to get the pharmacist?

    a) Claritin
    b) Zyrtec
    c) Benadryl
    d) Nasacort-Allergy 24 Hour

ANSWER.

A patient comes to the pharmacy counter with the following over-the-counter medicine and tells you they run a lawn care business and spend quite a bit of the day driving. Which medicine would cause you to get the pharmacist?

a) Claritin
b) Zyrtec
c) Benadryl
d) Nasacort-Allergy 24 Hour

Answer: C. Benadryl. While I there's not a true drug-occupation interaction, the patient needs allergy relief and a sedating medicine is concerning given the amount they drive. Let's look at why some of are safe and others not.

A. Claritin, generic loratadine has the atadine, -a-t-a-d-i-n-e stem that indicates it is a second-generation minimally sedating antihistamine. Since it doesn't cause a lot of drowsiness, this might have been a better choice.

B. Zyrtec, generic cetirizine, doesn't have a stem, but levocetirizine (Xyzal) are related second-generation antihistamines that are minimally sedating as well.

C. Benadryl, generic diphenhydramine, is a first-generation antihistamine which means there are many anticholinergic properties, and it makes the user very drowsy. The word bed, b-e-d is even in Bendadryl to help you remember.

D. Nasacort Allergy 24 HR, generic triamcinolone, has the -lone, l-o-n-e ending. Since the administration is intranasal and local to where the allergic rhinitis, that allergy inflammation occurs, side effects are much lower than an oral steroid. Steroids actually increase wakefulness.

QUESTION R25.

This pair constitutes a drug-disease interaction:

a) Albuterol-asthma.
b) Prednisone-diabetes.
c) Loratadine-hypertension.
d) Fluticasone-allergic rhinitis

ANSWER.

This pair constitutes a drug-disease interaction:

a) Albuterol-asthma.
b) Prednisone-diabetes.
c) Loratadine-hypertension.
d) Fluticasone-allergic rhinitis

Answer: B. Prednisone-diabetes. When we are looking at drug-disease interactions, we are looking for the most foundational issue in the disease, whether it is breathing, blood sugar levels, blood pressure, or inflammation.

Since the answers are all generic names, we can look quickly to see if there are recognizable prefixes and suffixes as well.

A. Albuterol-asthma - With asthma, we have inflammation and constriction of the lungs, so any drug that makes that worse would be a drug-disease interaction with asthma. Albuterol, a bronchodilator, opens or dilates the lungs, making asthma better, so this is not a drug-disease interaction, but a therapeutic interaction, one that helps the patient.

B. Prednisone-diabetes. Diabetes is a condition of hyperglycemia, or elevated glucose. As such, a drug like oral prednisone, that increases blood glucose to help the body get ready for fight or flight actually hurts the diabetic patient constituting a drug-disease interaction.

C. Loratadine-hypertension. This pair tests whether you know the difference between an antihistamine, like loratadine, with the -a-t-a-d-i-n-e stem that really doesn't have much effect on heart rate and blood pressure and a decongestant like pseudoephedrine, with the drine, d-r-i-n-e stem that does increase heart rate.

Not to get into the weeds on this one, but there is a formula that Cardiac Output = Heart Rate x Stroke Volume. We calculate stroke volume by subtracting the end-systolic volume from the end-diastolic volume.

Blood pressure components include systolic (on top) and diastolic (on bottom). Point is, watch for decongestants and blood pressure, not as much with antihistamines.

D. Fluticasone-allergic rhinitis is actually a therapeutic pairing. We see the sone, s-o-n-e ending, which is going to help an inflammation, an -itis, i-t-i-s. It is not a drug-disease interaction.

QUESTION R26.

A patient has fluticasone/salmeterol (Advair) a combination steroid with a bronchodilator. They've developed a hoarseness and white patchy tongue. What instruction do you expect the pharmacist to give to avoid this side effect?

   a) Rinse your mouth out with water after use
   b) Stop using until symptoms resolve
   c) Use a spacer to prevent these effects
   d) Contact your doctor about using oral steroids rather than inhaled steroids

ANSWER.

A patient has fluticasone/salmeterol (Advair) a combination steroid with a bronchodilator. They've developed a hoarseness and white patchy tongue. What instruction do you expect the pharmacist to give to avoid this side effect?

    a) **Rinse your mouth out with water after use**
    b) Stop using until symptoms resolve
    c) Use a spacer to prevent these effects
    d) Contact your doctor about using oral steroids rather than inhaled steroids

Answer: A. Rinse your mouth out with water after use.

A. Rinse your mouth out with water after [every] use is good advice as *Candida albicans,* or thrush can form with steroids. Steroids tend to reduce immunity which can be good if you want to keep a transplant patient's body from rejecting an organ or if you want to treat an autoimmune disease like rheumatoid arthritis. But when you locally suppress the immune system, an opportunistic yeast infection like thrush can form. It can also cause hoarseness.

B. Stop using until symptoms resolve. Your asthma hasn't gone away and stopping the medication for an extended period will allow attacks to return in greater quantities.

C. Use a spacer to prevent these effects might be good advice, but unfortunately Advair Diskus, Asmanex Twisthaler, and Pulmicort Flexhaler are three medications you shouldn't use a spacer with.

D. Contact your doctor about using oral steroids rather than inhaled steroids. Oral steroids can cause many chronic side effects and we don't want to move from a drug that has local effects to one that has systemic effects.

QUESTION R27.

Which medication would fall under the Combat Methamphetamine Epidemic Act of 2005?

    a) Aleve-D
    b) Aleve
    c) Allegra
    d) Afrin

ANSWER.

Which medication would fall under the Combat Methamphetamine Epidemic Act of 2005?

> **a) Aleve-D**
> b) Aleve
> c) Allegra
> d) Afrin

Answer: A. Aleve D.

A. Aleve by itself is a non-steroidal anti-inflammatory, naproxen. However, the -D letter suffix indicates decongestant. As such, Aleve-D is a combination of naprsxen sodium 220 mg and pseudoephedrine 120 mg in an extended-release tablet. Pseudoephedrine falls under the Combat Methamphetamine Epidemic Act of 2005.

B. Aleve by itself is the NSAID naproxen, not subject to this regulation.

C. Allegra, generic fexofenadine, is a minimally sedating antihistamine. However, if the answer was Allegra-D, then yes, like Aleve D it would fall under the Combat Methamphetamine Act of 2005.

D. Afrin, generic oxymetazoline is a decongestant, but it is a nasal spray and not one that could be turned into methamphetamine.

QUESTION R28.

Which of the following correctly pairs the generic and brand names of the medication?

   a) Loratadine (Zyrtec)
   b) Guaifenesin DM (Mucinex DM)
   c) Albuterol HFA (Flovent HFA)
   d) Montelukast (Nasonex)

ANSWER.

Which of the following correctly pairs the generic and brand names of the medication?

    a) Loratadine (Zyrtec)
    b) Guaifenesin DM (Mucinex DM)
    c) Albuterol HFA (Flovent HFA)
    d) Montelukast (Nasonex)

Answer: B. Guaifenesin DM (Mucinex DM)

A. Loratadine is a 2nd generation antihistamine, like Zyrtec, but Loratadine's brand name is Claritin and Zyrtec's generic name is cetirizine.

B. Guaifenesin DM (Mucinex DM) is the correct answer. I think of green mucus connecting the g in guafenesin DM with the m in Mucinex DM.

C. Albuterol HFA has a brand name of ProAir HFA and Flovent HFA has a generic name of fluticasone HFA. They are both for asthma, but albuterol is a bronchodilator and fluticasone is an inhaled steroid.

D. Montelukast has a brand name of Singulair. Montelukast has the mon, m-o-n from "mono, m-o-n-o" meaning "on"e and Singulair has most of the word single, also meaning one and the correct dosing schedule. Brand Nasonex has a generic of mometasone, and the letters n and m are only one apart in the alphabet.

QUESTION R29.

You would classify the following as an antitussive?

a) Dextromethorphan
b) Guaifenesin
c) Diphenhydramine
d) Pseudoephedrine

Answer: A. Dextromethorphan. Despite the hundreds of cough and cold products, there are surprisingly few drug classes, around seven. You can think of deans of a college all having cold symptoms.

ANSWER.

You would classify the following as an antitussive?

a) **Dextromethorphan**
b) Guaifenesin
c) Diphenhydramine
d) Pseudoephedrine

Answer: A. Dextromethorphan. Despite the hundreds of cough and cold products, there are surprisingly few drug classes, around seven. You can think of deans of a college all having cold symptoms.

MNEMONIC – COLD SYMPTOM DEANS

D	Decongestants
E	Expectorants
A	Antihistamines and Antitussives
N	Non-narcotic analgesics and NSAIDs
S	Steroids

A. Dextromethorphan (Delsym) or the DM in Mucinex DM is an over-the-counter antitussive while codeine is by prescription only. This is the appropriate treatment for a non-productive cough.

B. Guaifenesin (Mucinex) or (Robitussin) is an expectorant often paired with a cough suppressant or antitussive.

C. Diphenhydramine and desloratadine, loratadine, cetirizine, levocetirizine, and fexofenadine are all antihistamines.

D. Decongestants include oral tablets like pseudoephedrine (Sudafed) and nasal decongestants like oxymetazoline (Afrin).

It wasn't an answer choice, but over the counter nasal steroids for allergic rhinitis include triamcinolone (Nasacort Allergy 24HR) or fluticasone (Flonase). The OTC non-narcotic analgesic is acetaminophen (Tylenol) and the OTC NSAIDs are ibuprofen (Advil, Motrin) and naproxen (Aleve).

QUESTION RD30.

A patient pays cash for their prescription for albuterol with 200 metered puffs and wants to know how long it should last them. They say they've only been using 2 puffs three times a day on average instead of the four times a day the doctor said they might need. How long, in days, will this single inhaler last the patient using 2 puffs three times daily?

   a) 22
   b) 33
   c) 66
   d) 90

ANSWER.

A patient pays cash for their prescription for albuterol with 200 metered puffs and wants to know how long it should last them. They say they've only been using 2 puffs three times a day on average instead of the four times a day the doctor said they might need. How long, in days, will this single inhaler last the patient using 2 puffs three times daily?

a) 22
b) 33
c) 66
d) 90

Answer: B, 33 days.

So, your first step should be to set up the fence or table and put in the label as the answer, in this case days per inhaler

			days
			inhaler

Write out the factors.

1 dose / 2 puffs | 1 day / 3 doses | 200 puffs / 1 inhaler

Then put the factors in:

200 puffs	1 dose	1 day	days
1 inhaler	2 puffs	3 doses	inhaler

And solve:

200 ~~puffs~~	1 ~~dose~~	1 day	33 days
1 inhaler	2 ~~puffs~~	3 ~~doses~~	1 inhaler

PRACTICE EXAM PART 4 IMMUNE AND INTEGUMENTARY

QUESTION 131.

Which drug program monitoring is associated with thalidomide, a drug that can endanger a fetus and has an indication for multiple myeloma?

a) REMS
b) iPledge
c) White blood cell count
d) MethCheck

ANSWER.

Which drug program monitoring is associated with thalidomide, a drug that can endanger a fetus and has an indication for multiple myeloma?

a) **REMS**
b) iPledge
c) White blood cell count
d) MethCheck

Answer: A. Thalomid REMS. In thinking about special considerations for certain medications, we have some definite must-know entities. To remember these medications, especially those REMS to prevent defects in pregnancy, you can use the SUBUTOPIC mnemonic. Often, REMS is a subtopic after you've completed the traditional work on therapeutic indication, etc.

MNEMONIC – REMS PROGRAM MEDS – SUBTOPIC

SU	Decongestants
B	Expectorants
T	Antihistamines and Antitussives
O	Non-narcotic analgesics and NSAIDs
P	Steroids
I	Isotretinoin
C	Clozapine

A. Thalomid REMS is an R, Risk, E, Evaluation, and M, mitigation, S, Strategy. The risk came from its use back in the late 50s and 60s for nausea in pregnancy women. Unfortunately, that treatment led to thousands of children with terrible birth defects including phocomelia, which literally translates to seal limbs. This shortening of the limbs led to thalidomide's ban in many countries, but because of

87

its effectiveness against cancer led to its use under the REMS program, despite the pregnancy risks. The phentermine/topiramate (Qsymia), REMS is meant to avoid congenital malformations including orofacial clefts in infants exposed to Qsymia during the first trimester.

B. Isotretinoin is under the iPledge program, as patients as asked to pledge to do everything they can to prevent pregnancy as the chance of birth defects is very high. There are a number of brand names under this program in addition to isotretinoin generic including Absorica, Absorica LD, Amnesteem, Claravis, Myorisan, and Zenatane.

C. White blood cell count usually refers to clozapine (Clozaril) where white blood cell counts need to be carefully monitored. A form of olanzapine (Zyprexa Relprevv) can have very of with post-injection delirium/sedation syndrome (PDSS) and this program works to avoid them.

D. MethCheck tracks the amount of pseudoephedrine consumers are buying and blocks sales that exceed certain limits. However, buprenorphine (Suboxone) and naloxone/buprenorphine (Subutex) have a REMS program to help prevent accidental overdose, misuse and abuse.

QUESTION I32.

Which brand name medication contains a long-acting inhaled steroid?

a) Symbicort
b) ProAir HFA
c) Spiriva Respimat
d) Tamiflu

ANSWER.

Which brand name medication contains a long-acting inhaled steroid?

      a) Symbicort
      b) ProAir HFA
      c) Spiriva Respimat
      d) Tamiflu

Answer: A. Symbicort. As you continue with practice questions, you'll see that often an answer is one or two levels hidden. Just like in practice, catching a potential error will take a little bit of extra brain power.

A. Symbicort includes two medicines, budesonide and formoterol, like and like is Advair, a steroid/bronchodilator combination. You can see the son, s-o-n infix representing a steroid. While the question didn't ask for this, knowing that the terol, t-e-r-o-l is a bronchodilator will come in handy.

B. ProAir HFA is albuterol, again with the terol, t-e-r-o-l stem, indicating it is a bronchodilator, not a steroid.

C. Spiriva Respimat's generic is tiotropium, with the tropium, t-r-o-p-i-u-m anticholinergic ending. Usually these are also for COPD in addition to asthma.

D. Tamiflu is oseltamivir, with the amivir, a-m-i-v-i-r ending indicating it is not just an antiviral, but one for influenza as the brand name alludes to "taming the flu."

QUESTION I33.

The auxiliary label to not drink alcoholic beverages would be on which medication?

a) Metronidazole
b) Fluconazole
c) Acyclovir
d) Sulfamethoxazole

ANSWER.

The auxiliary label to not drink alcoholic beverages would be on which medication?

    a) **Metronidazole**
    b) Fluconazole
    c) Acyclovir
    d) Sulfamethoxazole

Answer: A. Metronidazole.

A. Metronidazole's brand name is Flagyl and you can think of a Flagon of ale or wine as a way to remember the alcohol connection. It will produce the disulfiram reaction of severe nausea and vomiting in combination. Disulfiram (Antabuse) is to help with alcohol abuse and just like the brand name sounds, it's against the abuse of alcohol.

B. Fluconazole, an antifungal does not have this issue.

C. Acyclovir (Zovirax) also does not have a vomiting reaction to alcohol.

D. Sulfamethoxazole / Trimethoprim (Bactrim) is an antibiotic and while patients shouldn't really drink while they are sick, it does not produce a disulfiram effect.

QUESTION 134.

Patients allergic to cephalosporins should avoid which medication?

   a) Keflex
   b) Vancocin
   c) Doryx
   d) Cipro

ANSWER.

Patients allergic to cephalosporins should avoid which medication?

    a) Keflex
    b) Vancocin
    c) Doryx
    d) Cipro

Answer: A. Keflex. Often a drug class question is actually a generic brand question in disguise. When we open up the question with generic questions we see that there is one drug that is clearly a cephalosporin.

A. Keflex, cephalexin, with the ceph, cef prefix of cephalosporins, the correct answer.

B. Vancocin, vancomycin, with the mycin, m-y-c-i-n suffix.

C. Doryx, doxycycline, with the cycline, c-y-c-l-i-n-e stem of tetracycline antibiotics.

D. Cipro, ciprofloxacin, with the floxacin, f-l-o-x-a-c-i-n stem of fluoroquinolone antibiotics.

QUESTION 135.

A prescriber writes for two weeks of amoxicillin/clavulanic acid suspension which requires two bottles of medication. The patient only receives one reconstituted vial at checkout and is told to come back in a week. Why?

- a) Amoxicillin has a 14-day expiration, but it will be fresher if they return in a week
- b) Clavulanic acid has a shelf life of only 7 days once reconstituted
- c) Amoxicillin only has a shelf life of 7 days while reconstituted
- d) This suspension only has a 10-day shelf life once reconstituted

ANSWER.

A prescriber writes for two weeks of amoxicillin/clavulanic acid suspension which requires two bottles of medication. The patient only receives one reconstituted vial at checkout and is told to come back in a week. Why?

 a) Amoxicillin has a 14-day expiration, but it will be fresher if they return in a week
 b) Clavulanic acid has a shelf life of only 7 days once reconstituted
 c) Amoxicillin only has a shelf life of 7 days while reconstituted
 d) **This suspension only has a 10-day shelf life once reconstituted**

Answer: D. This suspension only has a 10-day shelf life once reconstituted. Every once in a while a prescriber will ask for a two-week regimen for an antibiotic that has a shelf life that is a little bit lower.

QUESTION 136.

A patient needed to use an EpiPen the last time they received ciprofloxacin. As such, you would place which antibiotic class in their profile as a severe allergy?

   a) Penicillins
   b) Macrolides
   c) Quinolones
   d) Aminoglycosides

ANSWER.

A patient needed to use an EpiPen the last time they received ciprofloxacin. As such, you would place which antibiotic class in their profile as a severe allergy?

 a) Penicillins
 b) Macrolides
 c) **Quinolones**
 d) Aminoglycosides

Answer: C. Quinolones.

A, penicillins include medications that end in cillin, c-i-l-l-i-n such as amoxicillin and ampicillin.

B, macrolides generally end in -thromycin, -t-h-r-o-m-y-c-i-n.

C, quinolones end in -floxacin, f-l-o-x-a-c-i-n and this matches ciprofloxacin, the correct answer.

D, aminoglycosides, like amikacin or tobramycin end in kacin, k-a-c-i-n or mycin, m-y-c-i-n.

QUESTION I37.

Red man syndrome is a possibility when we see a patient on which antibiotic?

a) Vancomycin
b) Clarithromycin
c) Tobramycin
d) Erythromycin

ANSWER.

Red man syndrome is a possibility when we see a patient on which antibiotic?

    a) Vancomycin
    b) Clarithromycin
    c) Tobramycin
    d) Erythromycin

Answer: A. Vancomycin.

A. Vancomycin is a glycopeptide antibiotic. There are a number of severe, unusually named side effects with some medications, this is one of them to remember. One way to put it in your brain is think vancomycin, mancomycin to remember red-man syndrome as a possible side effect.

B. Clarithromycin is often associated with a metallic taste rather than red man syndrome.

C. Tobramycin, and other aminoglycosides, are often associated with ototoxicity to the ear and renal toxicity to the kidney.

D. Erythromycin is more associated with GI upset.

QUESTION I38.

Penicillin allergic patients should avoid which of the following combination medications?

a) Advair
b) Augmentin
c) Bactrim
d) Symbicort

ANSWER.

Penicillin allergic patients should avoid which of the following combination medications?

    a) Advair
    b) Augmentin
    c) Bactrim
    d) Symbicort

Answer: B. Augmentin. The key to this question is expanding to get the generic names and seeing that two medications are not even antibiotics.

A. Advair is fluticasone/salmeterol, a steroid/bronchodilator combination.

B. Augmentin is a clavulanic acid/amoxicillin combination that includes a penicillin and is the correct answer.

C. Bactrim is a sulfamethoxazole/trimethoprim combination.

D. Symbicort includes two medicines, budesonide and formoterol, like Advair, a steroid/bronchodilator combination.

QUESTION 139.

This class of medications which can actually cause cancer, would be classified as hazardous.

a) Antibiotic
b) Antifungal
c) Antineoplastic
d) Neosporin

ANSWER.

This class of medications which can actually cause cancer, would be classified as hazardous.

> a) Antibiotic
> b) Antifungal
> **c) Antineoplastic**
> d) Neosporin

Answer: C. Antineoplastic.

A. While antibiotics used long term might increase cancer risk, they are not considered a hazardous drug class.

B. Antifungals are important as many of the cancer treatments lead to opportunistic fungi taking hold and some are life threatening, but it is the fungus, not the antifungal that is the hazard.

C. Antineoplastic is correct. A neoplasm is a new growth, but we often use antineoplastic as a synonym for anticancer drug. The irony is that some of the anticancer drugs can cause cancer and are quite dangerous and hazardous. The list's name is the National Institute for Occupational Safety and Health (NIOSH) List of Antineoplastic and Other Hazardous Drugs in Healthcare Settings, kind of giving the answer away.

D. Neosporin is a bacitracin/neomycin/polymyxin B over-the-counter antibiotic ointment. An over-the-counter preparation would never be hazardous.

QUESTION ID40.

A patient struggles to swallow pills and needs 500 mg of amoxicillin q 8 h for 14 days. How much Amoxicillin 250 mg/5 mL suspension in 150 mL bottles how many bottles will you dispense?

    a) 2
    b) 3
    c) 4
    d) 5

ANSWER.

A patient struggles to swallow pills and needs 500 mg of amoxicillin q 8 h for 14 days. How many Amoxicillin 250 mg/5 mL suspension in 150 mL bottles will you dispense?

        a) 2
        b) 3
        c) 4
        d) 5

Answer: C. 3. I would consider doing this in two steps, but the basics are still the same. However, some conversion factors may not be as readily apparent. I would use these two first: | 3 doses / day | 500 mg / dose |

Then setup a smaller fence to figure out milligrams.

14 days	3 doses	500 mg	21,000 mg
	day	dose	

Then setup a second fence with the other conversion factors:

| 250 mg / 5 mL |150 mL / 1 bottle |

21000 mg	5 mL	1 bottle	2.8 bottles
	250 mg	150 mL	

Now that I have that I need 2.8 bottles, I would have to round up a bit as there is no partial bottle when you are dispensing these kinds of prescriptions so 3 bottles is the answer.

PRACTICE EXAM PART 5
NEURO/PSYCH

QUESTION N41.

The medication most likely use for depression would be which of the following?

a) Selegiline
b) Simvastatin
c) Salmeterol
d) Sertraline

ANSWER.

The medication most likely use for depression would be which of the following?

       a) Selegiline
       b) Simvastatin
       c) Salmeterol
       d) Sertraline

Answer: D. Sertraline. Let's look at brand names to point us to the therapeutic use of the medications. Manytimes test makers will make C or D the answer for which of the following or WOTF questions forcing you to read through all of them or use the same first letter answers.

A. Selegiline has the -giline, g-i-l-i-n-e stem indicating a monoamine oxidase inhibitor (MAOI) type B and has two brand names, Eldepryl and Zelapar. The Eldepryl has the first letters of elderly and the p-r from Parkinson's disease, Zelapar also has the first three letters from Parkinson's.

B. Simvastatin has the -vastatin, v-a-s-t-a-t-i-n stem indicating an HMG CoA reductase inhibitor for cholesterol lowering. The brand name Zocor has cor, c-o-r from coronary indicating it is a cardiovascular medication.

D. Salmeterol's brand Serevent has the vent, v-e-n-t of many of the asthma inhalers.

D. Sertraline, with the antidepressant -traline stem is one way to recognize the medication. Zoloft elevates or "lofts" your mood. As such, this is the correct answer.

QUESTION N42.

Which medication can be effective for smoking cessation?

a) Effexor XR
b) Paxil CR
c) Ambien CR
d) Wellbutrin SR

ANSWER.

Which medication can be effective for smoking cessation?

    a) Effexor XR
    b) Paxil CR
    c) Ambien CR
    d) Wellbutrin SR

Answer: D. Wellbutrin SR. Let's pull apart brand names, add generics, and look at acronyms to get a full picture.

A. Effexor XR is venlafaxine XR, a serotonin-norepinephrine reuptake inhibitor (SNRI) antidepressant. The XR stands for extended release which means it lasts longer. The brand name Effexor alludes to its "effex" of better moods.

B. Paxil CR is paroxetine CR, a selective serotonin reuptake inhibitor (SSRI) antidepressant, the CR stands for controlled release. The pax, p-a-x in Paxil means "peace" in Latin, and alludes to the peace one receives from depression.

C. Ambien CR is zolpidem CR, a sedative-hypnotic. The brand Ambien speaks to an ambient environment for and the z in zolpidem goes with getting your z's in sleep.

D. Wellbutrin SR is bupropion SR, an atypical antidepressant that doesn't fit well in other classes. The SR stands for sustained release, and works for someone who is trying to quit smoking. The manufacturer added another brand name – Zyban, as in banning smoking.

It can interfere with sleep, so the first dose should be before 9 AM ensuring the second dose isn't after 5 PM. Some people take it for 2, 3 or even 6 months, but benefits of quitting smoking are enormous.

QUESTION N43.

Prozac and Serafem have an identical generic, which is it?

a) Duloxetine
b) Fluoxetine
c) Paroxetine
d) Atomoxetine

ANSWER.

Prozac and Serafem have an identical generic, which is it?

a) Duloxetine
b) Fluoxetine
c) Paroxetine
d) Atomoxetine

Answer: B. Fluoxetine. While it would be simple to say fluoxetine is generic, we want to address that we've got choices from three different classes all ending in oxetine, o-x-e-t-i-n-e but duloxetine is an SNRI, fluoxetine and paroxetine are SSRIs, and atomoxetine is for ADHD.

A. Duloxetine has two brand names, Cymbalta and Irenka, and is a serotonin-norepinephrine reuptake inhibitor usually for depression. However, it's also useful for anxiety, diabetic peripheral neuropathy (numbness, weakness, and pain from nerve damage often in the hands and feet), and fibromyalgia, pain and stiffness in the muscles. The "du, d-u" from duo indicates the two neurotransmitters it affects.

B. Fluoxetine's brand names are Prozac and Sarafem and is a selective-serotonin reuptake inhibitor generally for depression. However, when fluoxetine received the okay for pre-menstrual dysphoric disorder, the company added Sarafem as a brand name to give specific instructions to the patient in separate packaging. Serafem is like Seraphim, an angel for those who take it.

C. Paroxetine's brand name is Paxil, with the pax, p-a-x meaning peace from depression.

D. Atomoxetine is a non-stimulant for ADHD with Strattera as its brand name which takes letters from the words straighten attention.

QUESTION N44

Which of the following medications is an antipsychotic with a dosage form that lasts 2 weeks?

a) Ramelteon
b) Risperdal M-Tab.
c) Risperdal Consta
d) Risedronate

ANSWER.

Which of the following medications is an antipsychotic with a dosage form that lasts 2 weeks?

a) Ramelteon
b) Risperdal M-Tab.
c) Risperdal Consta
d) Risedronate

Answer: C. Risperdal Consta. One class of medications that benefits from a very long-acting form is the antipsychotic class as patients only need an injection every few weeks.

A. Ramelteon is generic for Rozerem, you can see the REM, R-E-M for rapid-eye movement sleep in the brand name. Roze also rhymes with doze.

B. Risperdal M-Tab is orally disintegrating risperidone.

C. Risperdal Consta cuts off the end of the word constant as this medicinely constantly works for two weeks and is correct. You can remember many of the long-acting antipsychotics with the PRO HARP mnemonic.

Mnemonic – Antipsychotic Injectibles PRO HARP

P	Paliperidone (Invega Sustenna, Invega Trinza)
R	Risperidone (Risperdal Consta)
O	Olanzapine (Zyprexa Relprevv)
H	Haloperidol (Haldol)
AR	Aripiprazole (Abilify Maintena)
P	Prolixin (generic is fluphenazine)

D. Risedronate has the -dronate, d-r-o-n-a-t-e ending of a bisophosphonate for osteoporosis, it is not for psychosis.

QUESTION N45.

Which pair represents a significant drug-food interaction?

a) Isocarboxazid and aged cheese
b) Paroxetine and grapefruit juice
c) Fluoxetine and kale
d) Duloxetine and milk

ANSWER.

Which pair represents a significant drug-food interaction?

a) **Isocarboxazid and aged cheese**
b) Paroxetine and grapefruit juice
c) Fluoxetine and kale
d) Duloxetine and milk

Answer: A. Isocarboxazid and aged cheese is a classic interaction, the other foods can have interactions, but not with the drugs listed.

A. Isocarboxazid is the generic for Marplan and patients taking this monoamine oxidase inhibitor (MAOI) should "plan" to avoid aged cheese, Chianti wine, and other tyramine containing foods.

B. Paroxetine does not interact with grapefruit juice, however, simvastatin, an HMG-CoA for cholesterol does.

C. Fluoxetine does not interact with kale, but warfarin, brand Coumadin does.

D. Duloxetine does not interact with milk, but fluoroquinolones and tetracyclines do.

QUESTION N46.

The brand names Wellbutrin and Zyban can both represent which generic medication?

a) Buspirone
b) Bupropion
c) Buprenorphine
d) Budesonide

ANSWER.

The brand names Wellbutrin and Zyban can both represent which generic medication?

a) Buspirone
b) Bupropion
c) Buprenorphine
d) Budesonide

Answer: B. Bupropion. While it may be easy to pick out a generic name when the other choices have different letters, sometimes a test maker can test look-alike/sound-alike by putting two in the same question.

A. Buspirone's brand name is Buspar, for anxiety. But it's generic name can use FDA approved tall-man letters in the middle capitalizing the PIR, P-I-R in busPIRone and capitalizing the PROP, P-R-O-P in buPROPion.

B. Buspropion is the correct answer, the generic of both Wellbutrin and Zyban, but the real test was differentiating this drug name between the other choices that all start with bu, b-u.

C. Buprenorphine is Subutex, an opioid partial agonist to help with opioid addiction keeping weaker effects than methadone. It has the orphine, o-r-p-h-i-n-e similar to morphine.

D. Budesonide has the son, s-o-n of a steroid and it's brand name Pulmicort combines pulmonary, for lungs, and cort, from corticosteroid.

QUESTION N47.

Which of the following is a generic benzodiazepine useful for anxiety?

a) Alendronate
b) Albuterol
c) Alprazolam
d) Alfuzosin

ANSWER.

Which of the following is a generic benzodiazepine useful for anxiety?

    a) Alendronate
    b) Albuterol
    c) Alprazolam
    d) Alfuzosin

Answer: C. Alprazolam. We can look at stems and a mnemonic to better remember alprazolam.

A. Alendronate is Fosamax, for osteoporosis with the dronate, d-r-o-n-a-t-e stem.

B. Albuterol is ProAir HFA with the terol, t-e-r-o-l stem of a bronchodilator.

C. Alprazolam is Xanax which has many letters of the word anxiety and the -azolam stem. A mnemonic we can use is OFT CALMED as benzodiazepines often calm the patient.

MNEMONIC – BENZODIAZEPINES – OFT CALMED

O	Oxazepam (Serax)
F	Flurazepam (Dalmane)
T	Triazolam (Halcion), Temazepam (Restoril)
C	Clonazepam (Klonopin)
A	Alprazolam (Xanax)
L	Lorazepam (Ativan)
M	Midazolam (Versed)
E	Estazolam (ProSom)
D	Diazepam (Valium)

D. Alfuzosin, brand name Uroxatral, alludes to urinary.

QUESTION N48.

Which medication would be least likely to cause diarrhea?

a) Zoloft
b) Augmentin
c) Glucophage
d) Trimox

ANSWER.

Which medication would be least likely to cause diarrhea?

  a) Zoloft
  b) Augmentin
  c) Glucophage
  d) Trimox

Answer: D. Trimox. While it's unusual to see a "which does not" question, it would be nice if we could magically bring those to the front of our brain with the MAGICS mnemonic.

MNEMONIC – DRUGS THAT CAUSE DIARRHEA - MAGICS

M	Magnesium hydroxide (Milk of Magnesia)
A	Amoxicillin/Clavulanic Acid (Augmentin)
G	Glucophage (generic is metformin)
I	Ibuprofen (Advil, Motrin)
C	Colchicine (ColCrys)
S	Sertraline (Zoloft), an SSRI

A. Zoloft, generic sertraline, is sometimes colloquially called squirtraline referring to the diarrhea that can occur.

B. Augmentin, the clavulanic acid in the combination medication with amoxicillin and clavulanic acid is the culprit causing diarrhea.

C. Glucophage is metformin, an antidiabetic, known for its fishy smell and almost immediate GI upset. Starting patients with lower doses can help.

D. Trimox, is amoxicillin alone. It's close relative ampicillin, and partner in Augmentin, clavulanic acid are the real GI upset causing culprits, so this is correct.

QUESTION N49.

The manufacturer's expiration date on carbamazepine reads without a day, only the month of January and a year. What is the last day that can be used?

a) January 1st
b) January 31st.
c) December 1st
d) December 31st

ANSWER.

The manufacturer's expiration date on carbamazepine reads without a day, only the month of January and a year. What is the last day that can be used?

    a) January 1st
    b) January 31st.
    c) December 1st
    d) December 31st

Answer: B. January 31st. A medication without a 1 to 31 day in the month is assumed to be good until the last day in that month.

QUESTION ND50.

With phenytoin 125mg/5mL, the prescriber asks for 1 teaspoonful three times daily. How many mL would a patient need for 30 days supply?

a) 120 mL
b) 300 mL
c) 450 mL
d) 600 mL

ANSWER.

With phenytoin 125mg/5mL, the prescriber asks for 1 teaspoonful three times daily. How many mL would a patient need for 30 days supply?

      a) 120 mL
      b) 300 mL
      c) 450 mL
      d) 600 mL

Answer: C. 450mL.

Let's list our conversion factors.

| 5 mL / 1 teaspoonful | 3 teaspoonfuls / day |

Let's start by putting our fence up with mL at the end and 30 days at the beginning.

30 days			mL

Then let's take our conversion factors and put them in.

30 days	3 tsp	5 mL	mL
	1 day	1 tsp	

Then solve by multiplying 30 days x 3 teaspoonfuls / day x 5 mL / teaspoonful to make 450 mL

30 days	3 tsp	5 mL	450 mL
	1 day	1 tsp	

PRACTICE EXAM PART 6
CARDIO

QUESTION C51.

A patient's profile shows omeprazole, ibuprofen, albuterol, and torsemide, which prescription represents a therapeutic duplication?

a) Lasix
b) Zithromax
c) Dilantin
d) Zestril

ANSWER.

A patient's profile shows omeprazole, ibuprofen, albuterol, and torsemide, which prescription represents a therapeutic duplication?

e) Lasix
f) Zithromax
g) Dilantin
h) Zestril

Answer: A. Lasix. As soon as we see multiple medications in a patient's chart, we definitely want to outline the suffixes and add the brand names.

A. Lasix, furosemide, with the semide, s-e-m-i-d-e stem, a loop diuretic. This ending is the same as torsemide, another loop diuretic and the therapeutic duplication.

B. Zithromax, azithromycin, with the thromycin, t-h-r-o-m-y-c-i-n ending of a macrolide antibiotic.

C. Dilantin is phenytoin, with the toin, t-o-i-n stem of an anticonvulsant.

D. Zestril is lisinopril, with the pril, p-r-i-l suffix of an angiotensin converting enzyme inhibitor, an ACEI.

QUESTION C52.

Which example is most likely triggering a *patient* Drug Utilization Review (DUR)?

a) Vasotec and Zestril together
b) Using brand Zestril
c) A male patient taking sildenafil
d) A price above $2000

ANSWER.

Which example is most likely triggering a *patient* Drug Utilization Review (DUR)?

> **a) Vasotec and Zestril together**
> b) Using brand Zestril
> c) A male patient taking sildenafil
> d) A price above $2000

Answer: A. Vasotec and Zestril together.

A. Using the generic names of Vasotec, enalapril, and Zestril, lisinopril, we see an identical -pril, p-r-i-l ending, a therapeutic duplication, one of seven common DURs. You can use the WIND DATA mnemonic as in, you are getting wind of a possible medication error or concern.

MNEMONIC – DRUG UTILIZATION REVIEW REASONS - WIND DATA

W	Wrong dosage, Incorrect dosage
IN	Interaction, Drug-drug interaction
D	Disease, Drug-disease
D	Duration, Incorrect duration
A	Allergy, Drug-allergy
T	Therapeutic duplication
A	Abuse, Misuse or abuse of medication

B. Using brand Zestril is not an issue, it may cost more.

C. A male patient taking sildenafil, Viagra, is consistent with its use.

D. A price above $2,000, while a significant expense, does not trigger a drug utilization review for a patient.

QUESTION C53.

A statin cholesterol medication has the NDC 00071-0155-40. To ensure the correct medication, a technician would verify that which number matches the stock bottle?

    a) 00071
    b) 0155
    c) 40
    d) There is not enough information given

ANSWER.

A statin cholesterol medication has the NDC 00071-0155-40. To ensure the correct medication, a technician would verify that which number matches the stock bottle?

      a) 00071
      b) 0155
      c) 40
      d) There is not enough information given

Answer: B. 0155. The easiest way to remember these is the MAP mnemonic.

MNEMONIC – NDC NUMBERS - MAP

M	Manufacturer
A	Actual product code
P	Package code

A. This first number, 00071 represents the manufacturer.

B. The second number, 0155, represents the actual product code and is the correct answer.

C. The third number, 40, represents the package code.

D. You can verify the medicine with the information given.

QUESTION C54.

Which of the following two cardiologic medications demonstrate the prescriber performed a therapeutic substitution?

a) Lipitor and atorvastatin
b) Zestril and lisinopril
c) Benicar and losartan
d) Lasix and furosemide

ANSWER.

Which of the following two cardiologic medications demonstrate the prescriber performed a therapeutic substitution?

        a) Lipitor and atorvastatin
        b) Zestril and lisinopril
        c) Benicar and losartan
        d) Lasix and furosemide

Answer: C. Benicar and losartan. In a therapeutic substitution, we expect to see the same stem, but not always. For example, sertraline and paroxetine are both SSRIs and ibuprofen and naproxen are both NSAIDs, however, we can expand all of the brand names to see if we can find matching stems.

A. Lipitor's generic name is atorvastatin, so this is a brand generic switch, not a therapeutic substitution.

B. Zestril's generic name is lisinopril, so this also is a brand, generic switch.

C. Benicar is olmesartan with the same -sartan, s-a-r-t-a-n ending as losartan. Both are Angiotensin II receptor blockers, ARBs and we can see by the similar ending marking this as the correct answer.

D. Lasix's generic name is furosemide, so this is a brand generic switch, not a therapeutic substitution.

QUESTION C55.

Which pair represents a drug-food interaction?

a) Atorvastatin and orange juice
b) Warfarin and kale
c) Ibuprofen and enoxaparin
d) Furosemide and Milk

ANSWER.

Which pair represents a drug-food interaction?

  a) Atorvastatin and orange juice
  b) Warfarin and kale
  c) Ibuprofen and enoxaparin
  d) Furosemide and Milk

Answer: B. Kale.

A. Lisinopril and broccoli are not a drug-food interaction, but it is with warfarin.

B. Warfarin has large amounts of vitamin K and will cause an interaction with warfarin. A patient on warfarin is trying to avoid clotting, but significant vitamin K will cause clotting.

C. Ibuprofen and enoxaparin is a drug-drug bleeding interaction. Make sure you are answer the question asked. The BLANCHED mnemonic can help you remember as someone who has lost blood will look pale or blanched.

MNEMONIC – DRUGS THAT CAUSE BLEEDING - BLANCHED

BL	Bleeding
A	Anticoagulants
N	NSAIDs
C	Clopidogrel, Coumadin
H	Heparin
E	Enoxaparin
D	DOACs – Direct oral anticoagulants

D. Furosemide and milk is not an interaction.

QUESTION C56.

Some medications require special packaging, which of the following should stay in its original container?

a) Lisinopril 20 mg tablets
b) Valsartan 40 mg tablets
c) Nitroglycerin 0.4 mg tablets
d) Digoxin 0.125 mg tablets

ANSWER.

Some medications require special packaging, which of the following should stay in its original container?

    a) Lisinopril 20 mg tablets
    b) Valsartan 40 mg tablets
    c) Nitroglycerin 0.4 mg tablets
    d) Digoxin 0.125 mg tablets

Answer: C. Nitroglycerin 0.4 mg tablets. While all of these medications can be for a cardiovascular patient, only nitroglycerin needs to stay in the original container. Sometimes, to get a label on the medicine, a technician may place the container in a vial, make sure it's an easy open lid. You don't want someone fumbling with a child-proof cap as they are having angina or chest pain.

QUESTION C57.

What dosing would a patient most likely take metoprolol tartrate?

    a) QD
    b) BID
    c) TID
    d) QID

ANSWER.

What dosing would a patient most likely take metoprolol tartrate?

   a) QD
   b) BID
   c) TID
   d) QID

Answer: B. BID. You can use the letter "T" from tartrate to remind you that this medication should be taken T, twice daily. Metoprolol tartrate's partner, metoprolol succinate has many of the letters from succinct, something smaller is succinct and this only requires a smaller number of doses, just one daily.

QUESTION C58.

Which might be a dangerous combination?

a) Lisinopril / HCTZ
b) Enalapril / HCTZ
c) Furosemide / K-DUR
d) Spironolactone / K-DUR

ANSWER.

Which might be a dangerous combination?

    a) Lisinopril / HCTZ
    b) Enalapril / HCTZ
    c) Furosemide / K-DUR
    d) Spironolactone / K-DUR

Answer: D. Spironolactone / K-DUR. With the answer choices, we see that potassium loss and gain is the focus. . Potassium chloride is a medication you want to keep an eye on. I think of the first three letters of the word IMProve safety or an IMP, a mischievious devil you want to watch.

MNEMONIC – HIGH ALERT MEDICATIONS – IMPROVE SAFETY

I	Insulin
M	Methotrexate
P	Potassium chloride

A. Lisinopril/HCTZ is actually a drug combination in brands Prinzide and Zestoretic, so a safe combination. Lisinopril causes potassium gain and HCTZ potassium loss which can even out.

B. Enalapril/HCTZ is also a drug combination in brand Vaseretic. Enalapril causes potassium gain and HCTZ potassium loss which can even out.

C. Furosemide, brand Lasix, can often cause a loss of potassium and potassium supplementation is common.

D. Spironolactone, Aldactone, is a potassium-sparing diuretic, one that actually increases potassium, so adding potassium would be dangerous.

QUESTION C59.

A prescription label recommends that the patient take the medication, HS, which medication would this most likely apply to?

    a) Furosemide
    b) Olmesartan
    c) Hydrochlorothiazide
    d) Triamterene

ANSWER.

A prescription label recommends that the patient take the medication, HS, which medication would this most likely apply to?

a) Furosemide
b) Olmesartan
c) Hydrochlorothiazide
d) Triamterene

Answer: B. Olmesartan as HS means hora somni in Latin, or at the hour of sleep and you want to take medications that cause fatigue or drowsiness at bedtime if possible.

But as we'll see, there are other reasons not to take the other drugs at night. Use the CLOZAPINE mnemonic to help remind you of those medications.

MNEMONIC - TAKE AT BEDTIME - CLOZAPINE

C	Citalopram (Celexa)
L	Lorazepam (Ativan) – benzodiazepines, in general
O	Olmesartan (Benicar) – ARBs, in general
Z	Zolpidem (Ambien), Zaleplon (Sonata)
A	Amitriptyline (Elavil)
P	Paroxetine (Paxil)
I	Imipramine (Tofranil)
N	aNtihistamines, 1st generation, like diphenhydramine
E	Enalapril, ACEIs, in general.

A. Furosemide, brand Lasix is a loop diuretic, taking a medication close to bedtime would often disrupt a patient's sleep with a need to urinate.

B. Olmesartan, brand Benicar, is an angiotensin II receptor blocker, that can cause dizziness and fatigue, which is less of an issue at bedtime.

C. Hydrochlorothiazide is a thiazide diuretic, also a problem taken at bedtime.

D. Triamterene is also a diuretic.

QUESTION CD60.

A pharmacy receives the following prescription:

Methylprednisolone 4 mg tablets
Disp: 6 days supply
Sig: 6 tabs PO day 1, 5 tabs PO day 2, 4 tabs PO day 3, 3 tabs
PO day 4, 2 tabs PO day 5, and 1 tab po day 6.

How many tablets will the pharmacy need to dispense for
this prescription?

    a) 14
    b) 21
    c) 24
    d) 42

ANSWER.

A pharmacy receives the following prescription:

Methylprednisolone 4 mg tablets
Disp: 6 days supply
Sig: 6 tabs PO day 1, 5 tabs PO day 2, 4 tabs PO day 3, 3 tabs
PO day 4, 2 tabs PO day 5, and 1 tab po day 6.

How many tablets will the pharmacy need to dispense for
this prescription?

    a) 14
    b) 21
    c) 24
    d) 42

Answer: B. 21. This is one of those dreaded prescriptions to
type out, but the math can actually be done with some
quick addition that sounds a lot like a rocket ship
countdown. I would take the extra minute to write out the
addition so as not to make a preventable mistake.

$6 + 5 + 4 + 3 + 2 + 1 = 21$ tablets.

PRACTICE EXAM PART 7 ENDOCRINE, ETC.

QUESTION E61.

Which of th following would be on the FDA approved list of generic drug names with Tall Man letters?

a) Metformin and methocarbamol
b) Prozac and Paxil
c) Zantac and Zetia
d) Glyburide and glipizide

ANSWER.

Which of th following would be on the FDA approved list of generic drug names with Tall Man letters?

a) Metformin and methocarbamol
b) Prozac and Paxil
c) Zantac and Zetia
d) Glyburide and glipizide

Answer: D. Glyburide and glipizide share many letters on the front and back and are on this list.

A. Metformin and methocarbamol have the same first two letters, but are significantly different besides.

B. Prozac and Paxil are brand names and would not be on the *generic* tall man letter list.

C. Zantac and Zetia are also brand names. Note, Zantac's new formulation which is no longer ranitidine, is famotidine, the same medication that is in Pepcid.

D. Glyburide and glipizide are on the list and share not only two letters in the front and three letters in the back, but also sound very much alike.

The tall man letters for glyburide would be BURIDE, B-U-R-I-D-E and the letters for glipizide are ZIDE, Z-I-D-E. Don't confuse tall man letter choices with drug stems like gly, g-l-y, and gli, g-l-i which are in front of drugs to help patients reduce glucose.

QUESTION E62.

Which of the following falls within a correct refrigerated insulin storage temperature for the pharmacy department?

   a) -10°C
   b) 7°C
   c) 25°C
   d) 30°C

ANSWER.

Which of the following falls within a correct refrigerated insulin storage temperature for the pharmacy department?

    a) -10°C
    b) 7°C
    c) 25°C
    d) 30°C

Answer: B. 7°C

A. -10°C is a frozen temperature, not a refrigerator temperature.

B. 7°C is a refrigerator temperature. Two ranges you absolutely want to remember are 2 to 8 °C is 36 to 46 °F. To memorize this, I would think I see (C), you too (2), ate (8) from the refrigerator to remember Celsius, and the 2- and 8-degree range. For farhenheit, I would look at the identical ending number in 36 and 46 F.

C. 25°C is the upper edge of where you want to see a room temperature medication from 20-25 °C and 68-77°F. To memorize this look at the same first number in 20 to 25 and I think of there being ROOM in the middle for 7 as the number between 6 and 8 to connect 68 and 77 as room temperature.

D. 30°C is where you usually see the word excursions, as in excursions permitted to 30°C or 86°F.

QUESTION E63.

Which medication would help provide relief from BPH?

a) Proscar
b) Glucophage
c) Synthroid
d) Urecholine

ANSWER.

Which medication would help provide relief from BPH?

   a) Proscar
   b) Glucophage
   c) Synthroid
   d) Urecholine

Answer: A. Proscar is for benign prostatic hyperplasia, BPH. Sometimes the struggle is just getting the acronyms down to make sure you have a complete understanding of the question.

A. Proscar as a brand name stands for prostate care, but one could also look at the steride, s-t-e-r-i-d-e suffix for testosterone reductase inhibitors.

B. Glucophage is metformin and we can see from the gluco, this has to do with glucose lowering.

C. Synthroid is synthetic thyroid for hypothyroid.

D. Urecholine is a cholinergic for urinary retention.

QUESTION E64.

A patient has to provide insulin to their grandparent, however, they found out the medication was left outside of the refrigerator. How long is this medication usually good for after removing it from the refrigerator?

a) 12 hours
b) 24 hours
c) 14 days
d) 28 days

ANSWER.

A patient has to provide insulin to their grandparent, however, they found out the medication was left outside of the refrigerator. How long is this medication usually good for after removing it from the refrigerator?

    a) 12 hours
    b) 24 hours
    c) 14 days
    d) 28 days

Answer: D. Mail order insulin comes in a box with many freezer bags to keep it cool. Many believe that the insulin has to be frozen or kept in the refrigerator or it will go bad. The mailed prescription is a way to maintain insulin for a much longer in the refrigerator time. Insulin left out of the refrigerator is usually good for 28 days, but most keep it in the refrigerator anyway.

QUESTION E65.

Which medication generally has a dosage in micrograms?

    a) Synthroid
    b) Flomax
    c) Humulin R
    d) K-DUR

ANSWER.

Which medication generally has a dosage in micrograms?

    a) Synthroid
    b) Flomax
    c) Humulin R
    d) K-DUR

Answer: A. Synthroid.

A. Synthroid usually expresses its dosages in micrograms, mcg. The idea is to avoid the decimal, so instead .2 mg, you will often see 200 mcg.

B. While Flomax does have a fraction of a milligram as a dosage, convention is to express it as Flomax .4 mg or .4 milligrams.

C. Humulin R and other insulins are expressed in units.

D. K-DUR, potassium chloride is expressed in milliequivalents.

QUESTION E66.

Which represents a significant drug interaction?

- a) Sildenafil and nitroglycerin
- b) Furosemide and potassium
- c) HCTZ and triamterene
- d) Sacubitril and valsartan

ANSWER.

Which represents a significant drug interaction?

a) Sildenafil and nitroglycerin
b) Furosemide and potassium
c) HCTZ and triamterene
d) Sacubitril and valsartan

Answer: A. Sildenafil and nitroglycerin.

A. Sildenafil and nitroglycerin is a classic and must-know drug interaction.

B. Furosemide actually reduces a body's potassium, so adding potassium is a good thing.

C. HCTZ and triamterene work together as a drug that reduces potassium and another that retains it to cancel the bad out.

D. Sacubitril and valsartan are a combination medication in Entresto. The brand name is one that indicates a patient should entrust their cardiovascular care to the medicine. Sacubitril is a neprilysin inhibitor combined with valsartan, an angiotensin II receptor blocker.

QUESTION E67.

The ultra-short acting insulin is:

a) Insulin lispro
b) Insulin regular
c) Insulin neutral protamine hagedorn (NPH)
d) Insulin glargine

ANSWER.

The ultra-short acting insulin is:

    a) **Insulin lispro**
    b) Insulin regular
    c) Insulin neutral protamine hagedorn (NPH)
    d) Insulin glargine

Answer: A. Insulin lispro. To memorize the order of insulins and their speed of action from ultra-short acting to regular to intermediate to long-acting use the LEARNING mnemonic and the order you find the L, lispro, R, regular, N, NPH, and G, glargine.

MNEMONIC – INSULIN SPEED OF ACTION – LEARNING

L	Lispro – ultra short-acting
E	
A	
R	Regular – short-acting
N	NPH – intermediate
I	
N	
G	Glargine, long-acting

QUESTION E68.

Which medication is for a severe hypoglycemic state?

a) Glucagon
b) Glyburide
c) Glipizide
d) Pioglitazone

ANSWER.

Which medication is for a severe hypoglycemic state?

    a) Glucagon
    b) Glyburide
    c) Glipizide
    d) Pioglitazone

Answer: A. Glucagon.

A. Use the mnemonic that you use Glucagon when the glucose is gone as in hypoglycemia, a shortage of glucose.

B. Glyburide is for diabetes, a hyperglycemic state.

C. Glipizide is for diabetes, a hyperglycemic state.

D. Pioglitazone is for diabetes, a hyperglycemic state.

QUESTION E69.

A patient takes their Lantus prescription home and uses their first dose. How long, in days, is this medication good for once opened?

a) 7
b) 14
c) 21
d) 28

ANSWER.

A patient takes their Lantus prescription home and uses their first dose. How long, in days, is this medication good for once opened?

    a) 7
    b) 14
    c) 21
    d) 28

Answer: D. 28 days. Just as an insulin can be out of the refrigerator for 28 days, once a patient starts on Lantus, insulin glargine, it must be discarded after 28 days. This is frustrating for diabetic cat owners who use very small doses and waste a lot of medicine.

If you look at the letter "L" at the beginning of Lantus and letter "S" at the end, the L has the tail of the number 2 and the S like a number 8 to help you remember Lantus is good for 28 days. Another way to remember it is that "Lantus glargine" has two words and 14 letters, 2 x 14 = 28.

QUESTION ED70.

How many days will a Lantus SoloStar U-100 Pen last if there are 3 mL in the pen and the patient uses 20 units a day?

    a) 15
    b) 30
    c) 45
    d) 60

ANSWER.

How many days will a Lantus SoloStar U-100 Pen last if there are 3 mL in the pen and the patient uses 20 units a day?

      a) 15
      b) 30
      c) 45
      d) 60

Answer: D. 15.

Let's start by putting our fence up with days at the end and 3 mL at the beginning.

3 mL			days

Then let's take our conversion factors:

100 Units / 1 mL which you must memorize.

20 Units / day from the problem.

and put them in.

3 mL	100 units	1 day	days
	1 mL	20 units	

Then solve

3 ~~mL~~	100 ~~units~~	1 day	15 days
	1 ~~mL~~	20 ~~units~~	

PRACTICE EXAM PART 8
DOSAGE CALCULATIONS

QUESTION D71.

A prescriber wants 2 mg per kg q.i.d. for a 220-pound patient. How many mg will the patient receive daily?

    a) 100
    b) 200
    c) 400
    d) 800

ANSWER.

A prescriber wants 2 mg per kg q.i.d. for a 220-pound patient. How many mg will the patient receive daily?

  a) 100
  b) 200
  c) 400
  d) 800

Answer: D. 800.

Let's start by putting our fence up with milligrams/day at the end and 220 pounds at the beginning so we have a clear picture of our starting and finishing line.

220 lbs				mg
				day

Let's get our conversion factors. I use what are called pipes (it's on your keyboard above the slash) to separate them.

2.2 lbs / 1 kg | 2 mg/kg/dose | 4 doses / day |

Now, some people like to figure out what the number of kilograms is in a separate equation, which is fine, but I'll show you how you can just make one single equation which makes it a lot easier to imagine in your mind's eye.

220 lbs	1 kg	2 mg	4 doses	mg
	2.2 lbs	kg / dose	day	day

Then solve:

220 lbs	1 kg	2 mg	4 doses	800 mg
	2.2 lbs	kg / dose	day	day

QUESTION D72.

A prescription arrives electronically at the pharmacy with the following instructions:

Sig: Two 250 mg tablets day one and then one tablet each day until all taken for four additional days

What is the dosage of the regimen?

a) 500 mg
b) 1000 mg
c) 1200 mg
d) 1500 mg

ANSWER.

A prescription arrives electronically at the pharmacy with the following instructions:

Sig: Two 250 mg tablets day one and then one tablet each day until all taken for four additional days

What is the dosage of the regimen?

a) 500 mg
b) 1000 mg
c) 1200 mg
d) 1500 mg

Answer: D. 1500 mg.

You might recognize this as a Zithromax Z-Pak, but you'll be amazed at how many people put 5 tablets and then calculate milligrams incorrectly. Before we solve this, let's to answer another question you might see. Note, the first two tablets are a loading dose meant to get the drug levels above a certain range.

How many milligrams did the patient get in total? There's nothing wrong with adding 2 + 1 + 1 + 1 + 1 = 6 to get the number of tablets they got in the regimen. You could do ((2 *1) + (4*1)) = 6, but that seems like you could make a mistake in that parenthesis madness. You do parenthesis first, multiplication, then addition. Once you know you need six tablets, set up the equation and solve.

6 tablets	250 mg	1500 mg
	1 tablet	day

QUESTION D73.

How many milligrams will a patient be able to get from a
120 mL bottle of ibuprofen that has 100 mg/teaspoonful?

a) 800
b) 1600
c) 2400
d) 3200

ANSWER.

How many milligrams will a patient be able to get from a 120 mL bottle of ibuprofen that has 100 mg/teaspoonful?

a) 800
b) 1600
c) 2400
d) 3200

Answer: C. 2400. You'll need to have a few measures memorized, but the math is straightforward. Let's put our start and finish line on the fence though.

120 mL			mg

Then put in our factors.

| 5 mL / 1 tsp |100 mg / 5 mL |

120 mL	1 tsp	100 mg	mg
	5 mL	1 tsp	

And solve.

120 mL	1 tsp	100 mg	2400 mg
	5 mL	1 tsp	

QUESTION D75.

What percentage of drug product do you get when you combine 60 g of 5% ointment with 30 g of 2% ointment?

a) 0.044 %
b) 0.44 %
c) 4.44 %
d) 44.4 %

ANSWER.

What percentage of drug product do you get when you combine 60 g of 5% ointment with 30 g of 2% ointment?

    a) 0.044 %
    b) 0.44 %
    c) 4.44 %
    d) 44.4 %

Answer: C. 4.44%. There's actually a way to do this problem without doing any math at all. Many times the test makers will try to trick you on decimals and put the exact same numbers in with the decimal moving in each case. However, the 2% and 5% represent the minimum and maximum of the ointment percentage.

For example, if you have 2% milk and 1% milk, there is no combination of those two milks that can take you below 1% or above 2%. It's mathematically impossible. Since the only number that falls between 2 and 5 is 4.44, that's the answer, but let me show you how to do the match anyway.

The first thing I would recommend is to not use decimals in the conversion. Instead of trying to get the 0.02 and 0.05 by dividing 2% and 5% by 100, then I would recommend using that a percent of anything is that number over 100.

60 g	5 g active	3 g	
	100 g cream		
15 g	2 g active	.3 g	
	100 g cream		
75 g total ointment		3.3 g active	

3.3 active / 75 g total = .044 x 100 = 4.4% in the new ointment mixture.

PRACTICE EXAM PART 9
ACRONYMS AND
ABBREVIATIONS

QUESTION A76.

Where is a patient using a medication if the instructions indicate application "AS?"

a) Right eye
b) Left eye
c) Right ear
d) Left ear

ANSWER.

Where is a patient using a medication if the instructions indicate application "AS?"

a) Right eye
b) Left eye
c) Right ear
d) Left ear

Answer: D. Left ear. They key to learning Latin abbreviations is to connect it to something you know already, like binoculars for eyes and audiobooks for ears.

A. Right eye, OD, oculus dexter in Latin. The ocul, o-c-u-l from oculus, o-c-u-l-u-s is the same one that is in binoculars, b-i-n-o-c-u-l-a-r-s which has two eye pieces.

Dexter, d-e-x-t-e-r includes the first six letters from dexterity, which means skill with hands. However, most people are right-handed, so it is generally associated with right. So, think about using your right eye through the binoculars with your right hand (the skilled dexterous one) to recognize OD, O-D means right eye.

B. Left eye, OS, oculus sinister. Sinister comes from those being different, left-handed, being sinister. Now you can think about fumbling with those binoculars with your bad hand, your sinister left one to remember OS.

C. Right ear, AD, is auris dexter, with the auris, a-u-r-i-s being the same beginning as audio, sound you hear. So, if when you put your earbuds in to listen to an audiobook, you usually start with your right and dextrous hand.

D. Left ear, AS, is auris sinister, is fumbling with the sinister left hand that isn't quite as skilled and the correct answer for this question.

QUESTION A77.

The words "once a day" should be used instead of which of the following to indicate a single use daily?

a) qd
b) bid
c) tid
d) qid

ANSWER.

The words "once a day" should be used instead of which of the following to indicate a single use daily?

    a) qd
    b) bid
    c) tid
    d) qid

Answer: A. qd. This question begs us to translate these terms in a way that we can remember them.

A. qd creates a problem because if qd means once a day, then why does qid mean four times a day? They stand for different words. The qd is "quaque die" with the pronunciation of d-i-e as the letters D, then A in order. You are much more familiar with the other q from qid as quarter in die where you have four quarters in a dollar.

B. bid translates to bis in die, but just think of a bicycle with two wheels for twice a day.

C. tid translates to "ter in die," but think of a tricycle with three wheels.

D. qid is quarter in die, you can think of a quadrunner with four wheels or four quarters in a dollar. The important thing is to connect the language you don't know, with something in the language you do know.

QUESTION A78.

A theft occurred in a pharmacy and the DEA must be notified. What form would one use to make the official report?

a) Form 41
b) Form 106
c) Form 222
d) Form 224

ANSWER.

A theft occurred in a pharmacy and the DEA must be notified. What form would one use to make the official report?

    a) Form 41
    b) Form 106
    c) Form 222
    d) Form 224

Answer: B. 106.

To memorize these weird form numbers, I would do a little bit of simple math and move the numbers around using the DEA FORMS 5, 6, 7, 8, 9 mnemonic.

The numbers 41, 222, 106, 224, 225 sound like a quarterback before the center hikes the ball, but I might consider putting in the order that if you add the numbers, they add up to 5, 6, 7, 8, and 9. Form 41 is 4+1 = 5, Form 222 is 2 + 2 + 2 =6, Form 1 + 0 + 6 = 7, and so on. This puts them in order to make the word DOT for those first three forms to remember, Destory, Order, Theft for 41, 222, and 106.

Mnemonic – DEA FORMS – 5, 6, 7, 8, 9

5	Form 41 – Destroy Controlled Substances
6	Form 222 – Order/Transfer Schedule I and II
7	Form 106 – Theft Reporting
8	Form 224 – Application New – retail, hospital, and clinic
9	Form 225 – Application New – manufacturer, wholesaler, distributer, research

QUESTION A79.

In an accident, a bottle of cough syrup spills onto a counting tray with 30 oxycodone tablets on it. The tablets are now useless. What DEA form would the pharmacy use to get permission to destroy these unsaleable tablets?

a) 41
b) 106
c) 222
d) 224

ANSWER.

In an accident, a bottle of cough syrup spills onto a counting tray with 30 oxycodone tablets on it. The tablets are now useless. What DEA form would the pharmacy use to get permission to destroy these unsaleable tablets?

    a) 41
    b) 106
    c) 222
    d) 224

Answer: A. 41. DEA form 41 is what one would use to destroy controlled substances.

QUESTION A80.

The DEA must be alerted to the theft of controlled substances within how many days?

    a) 1
    b) 2
    c) 3
    d) 4

ANSWER.

The DEA must be alerted to the theft of controlled substances within how many days?

  a) 1
  b) 2
  c) 3
  d) 4

Answer: A. 1. The Code of Federal Regulations (CFR) insists that pharmacies notify DEA Field Office in one business day of theft or loss.

QUESTION A81.

Dr. Smith is an optometrist writes a prescription for a pain medication for a patient who had severe trauma to their eye. Which of the following could not be her DEA number?

a) MC3164895
b) MA3164895
c) BS3164895
d) MS3164895

ANSWER.

Dr. Smith is an optometrist writes a prescription for a pain medication for a patient who had severe trauma to their eye. Which of the following could not be her DEA number?

  a) MC3164895
  b) MA3164895
  c) BS3164895
  d) MS3164895

Answer: C. BS3164895. At first this looks like a question that will test your knowledge of the DEA number verification formula, but all it's really asking is if Dr. Smith is a mid-level practitioner (not a physician, dentist, or veterinarian) or a mid-level practitioner (NP, PA, optometrist).

A. MC3164895 – After marriage, a person might change their last name, but their DEA letter does not change, this could be valid.

B. MA3164895 – For the same reason, this could be valid.

C. BS3164895 – The first letter indicates a physician, dentist, or veterinarian, so this could not be the DEA number.

D. MS3164895 – This includes the optometrist's last first initial as the second letter.

To check if 3164895 is a valid number, you would add

3 + 6 + 8, the first, third, and fifth number to get 17

Then add 1 + 4 + 9, the second, fourth, and sixth number to get 14 which you multiply by two to get 28.

This makes 17 + 28 = 45. That one's digit 5 is the last number and a valid DEA number.

QUESTION A82.

A reverse distributer is in charge of properly disposing of pharmaceutical waste. Which organization would ensure their best practices?

   a) CDC
   b) DEA
   c) EPA
   d) TJC

ANSWER.

A reverse distributer is in charge of properly disposing of pharmaceutical waste. Which organization would ensure their best practices?

    a) CDC
    b) DEA
    c) EPA
    d) TJC

Answer: C. EPA. Let's unpack the acronyms and what their agencies do.

A. CDC, is the Center for Disease Control and Prevention and is the national United States public health agency.

B. DEA, is the Drug Enforcement Administration who fights drug trafficking and distribution in the United States.

C. EPA, is the Environmental Protection Agency that deals with environmental protection matters like pharmaceutical waste and is the correct answer.

D. TJC, is The Joint Commission, where "The" is part of the name like "The Ohio State University." It accredits health care programs and organizations.

QUESTION A83.

Which of the following cannot be therapeutically equivalent according to the FDA?

    a) A blue and green tablet
    b) A capsule and a tablet
    c) Two capsules made by different manufacturers
    d) Two tablets made by different manufacturers

ANSWER.

Which of the following cannot be therapeutically equivalent according to the FDA?

    a) A blue and green tablet
    b) A capsule and a tablet
    c) Two capsules made by different manufacturers
    d) Two tablets made by different manufacturers

Answer: B. A capsule and a tablet. Use the FAR, F-A-R mnemonic to remember this one.

MNEMONIC – THERAPEUTIC EQUIVALENCE – FAR

F	Form of dosage
A	Active ingredients
R	Route of administration

A. A blue and green tablet are both tablets, same form, can have the same active ingredients, and go by the same oral route.

B. A capsule and tablet violate the F, the form of the dosage.

C. Two capsules are the same forms, it does not matter that two companies make the capsules.

D. Two tablet are the same forms, it does not matter that two companies make the tablets.

QUESTION A84.

When the FDA orders a Class I medication recall, the patient will have been exposed to what level of harm?

a) Deadly
b) Temporary
c) Little to none
d) Level A

ANSWER.

When the FDA orders a Class I medication recall, the patient will have been exposed to what level of harm?

    a) **Deadly**
    b) Temporary
    c) Little to none
    d) Level A

Answer: A. Deadly. The way I would remember this is to use the Deadly Temperatures, Little Precipitation mnemonic where a situation with deadly temperatures and no rain is very dangerous. This helps you remember the order of the Class I, II, and III recalls as deadly, temporary, and little harm.

MNEMONIC – DRUG RECALLS - DEADLY TEMPERATURES, LITTLE PRECIPITATION

Deadly	Class I Recall
Temporary	Class II Recall
Little	Class III Recall
Precipitation	

QUESTION A85.

Which of the NDC's numbers are assigned by the FDA?

a) The first 5
b) The second 4
c) The third 2
d) All of the numbers are assigned by the FDA

ANSWER.

Which of the NDC's numbers are assigned by the FDA?

   a) The first 5
   b) The second 4
   c) The third 2
   d) All of the numbers are assigned by the FDA

Answer: A. The first 5. The other numbers are actually assigned by the manufacturer.

QUESTION A86.

The entire NDC number and lot number would be needed for which of the following?

a) A drug's recall
b) A drug's expiration
c) To verify receipt to inventory
d) To verify storage instructions

ANSWER.

The entire NDC number and lot number would be needed for which of the following?

    a) A drug's recall
    b) A drug's expiration
    c) To verify receipt to inventory
    d) To verify storage instructions

Answer: A. The drug's recall. When a drug recall happens, they are sometimes recalling the medicine, or sometimes certain batches of it. In the latter case, we need the lot number to know which batches to send back.

QUESTION A87.

The third set of numbers in an NDC represent which of the following?

a) The drug manufacturer
b) The drug itself
c) The drug dosage form
d) The drug color

ANSWER.

The third set of numbers in an NDC represent which of the following?

a) **The drug manufacturer**
b) The drug itself
c) The drug dosage form
d) The drug color

Answer: A. The drug dosage form which is made up by the manufacturer.

PRACTICE EXAM PART 10 LAW

QUESTION L88.

Law – A biennial complete controlled substance inventory is required by Title 21 of the CFR. How often does this occur?

  a) Every 6 months
  b) Every 12 months.
  c) Every 20 months
  d) Every 24 months

ANSWER.

Law – A biennial complete controlled substance inventory is required by Title 21 of the CFR. How often does this occur?

    a) Every 6 months
    b) Every 12 months.
    c) Every 20 months
    d) Every 24 months

Answer: D. Every 24 months. Really, there's only two reasonable answers, either biennial is twice a year or every other year. Biannual, is twice a year and Biennial is every two years. How do we remember the difference?

The letter "a" in biannual comes before the "e" in biennial in the alphabet, so that shorter one, the every 6 months twice a year, is biannual is how I remember it.

QUESTION L89.

Law – A pharmacy confirms receipt of a controlled medication on July 20th of 2022. They must keep a record of that receipt until what date?

   a) July 20th, 2023
   b) July 20th, 2024
   c) July 20th, 2027
   d) July 20th, 2032

ANSWER.

Law – A pharmacy confirms receipt of a controlled medication on July 20th of 2022. They must keep a record of that receipt until what date?

      a) July 20th, 2023
      b) July 20th, 2024
      c) July 20th, 2027
      d) July 20th, 2032

Answer: B. July 20th, 2024. The exam could have just as easily put the name of an actual controlled substance, but the records must be kept for 2 years. This could also fall under the DEA acronym if it was explicitly stated.

QUESTION L90

Law – A patient receives a Schedule IV prescription for a sedative-hypnotic, what medicine can be filled how many times?

a) Up to 5 times in 6 months
b) Up to 5 times in a year
c) It may not be refilled
d) It can be refilled PRN

ANSWER.

Law – A patient receives a Schedule IV prescription for a sedative-hypnotic, what medicine can be filled how many times?

 a) **Up to 5 times in 6 months**
 b) Up to 5 times in a year
 c) It may not be refilled
 d) It can be refilled PRN

Answer: A. Up to 5 times in 6 months.

We need to remember three different refill situations.

Schedule II is no refills. If you struggle to remember this, the number "two, t-w-o" has a letter "o" which looks like a zero.

Schedule III, IV, V is up to five (V) refills in six months. So the 3, 4, 5, 6 hopefully makes this easier to remember.

Not scheduled, not a limit on refills puts two "nots, n-o-t-s" together to help you remember.

PRACTICE EXAM PART 11
SUPPLEMENTS

QUESTION S91.

Pregnant mothers generally need which supplement before conception to help prevent anencephaly and bifida?

   a) Folic acid
   b) Vitamin C
   c) Vitamin D
   d) Vitamin E

ANSWER.

Pregnant mothers generally need which supplement before conception to help prevent anencephaly and bifida?

- **a) Folic acid**
- b) Vitamin C
- c) Vitamin D
- d) Vitamin E

Answer: A. Folic acid. The American College of Obstetricians and Gynecologists recommend folic acid before conception and during early pregnancy to reduce neural tube defects risk.

If you were wondering, an obstetrician basically helps with everything up until immediately after delivery, while a gynecologist helps with women's health issues. An OB-GYN encompasses both.

QUESTION S92.

A patient looking for valerian root would most likely be trying to treat which condition?

   a) Anxiety
   b) High cholesterol
   c) Prostate issues
   d) Urinary tract issues

ANSWER.

A patient looking for valerian root would most likely be trying to treat which condition?

a) **Anxiety**
b) High cholesterol
c) Prostate issues
d) Urinary tract issues

Answer: A. Anxiety. It's just easiest if I give you a mnemonic to remember the supplements and most likely reason someone would take them. I'm not saying any of these work, I'm just saying this is what they come in for and why. You can use the EPICARDIUM mnemonic. While I get the epicardium is the outer surface of the heart membrane, it just seemed appropriate to connect heart and herbals.

MNEMONIC – COMMON HERBALS - EPICARDIUM

E	Energy - CoQ 10
P	Prostate – Saw Palmetto
I	Immune – Echinacea, Elderberry, Ginseng
C	Cholesterol – Fish Oil, Garlic, Niacin
A	Anxiety – Valerian root
R	Respiratory – Peppermint
D	Depression – St John's Wort
I	Insomnia – Melatonin
U	Urinary tract – Cranberry
M	Memory – Ginkgo, Menopause – Black cohosh

QUESTION S93.

A patient receives an oral contraceptive, which supplement would be of most concern?

   a) St. John's Wort
   b) Echinacea
   c) Vitamin C
   d) Vitamin D

ANSWER.

A patient receives an oral contraceptive, which supplement would be of most concern?

    a) **St. John's Wort**
    b) Echinacea
    c) Vitamin C
    d) Vitamin D

Answer: A. St. John's Wort. Because patients often don't consult a medical provider with OTCs and herbals, it's really important to ask the patient if they are on any vitamins or supplements, many think these are not medicines and don't count, but with interactions, they do.

QUESTION S94.

With Saw Palmetto, we expect the patient is trying to self-treat which condition?

    a) BPH
    b) CHF
    c) ADHD
    d) RA

ANSWER.

With Saw Palmetto, we expect the patient is trying to self-treat which condition?

> **a) BPH**
> b) CHF
> c) ADHD
> d) RA

Answer: A. BPH, benign prostatic hyperplasia. Whether in your mind's eye or on paper, write out abbreviations to have a more complete picture.

A. BPH, benign prostatic hyperplasia, a prostate gland enlargement.

B. CHF, congestive heart failure, wher the heart either doesn't fill (diastolic pressure) or pump (systolic pressure) appropriately.

C. ADHD, Attention-deficit/hyperactivity disorder, is a concern with attention, hyperactivity and impulsive behaviors.

D. RA, Rhematoid arthritis, an inflammation of the joints caused by the immune system.

PRACTICE EXAM PART 12
OTHER QUESTIONS

QUESTION 095.

A technician is reporting to MedWatch, what likely happened?

a) A patient received 60 tablets instead of 30 tablets
b) A patient received their medication two days late
c) A patient lost their birth control medication and needed a replacement
d) An error happened between two similar generic medication bottles

ANSWER.

A technician is reporting to MedWatch, what likely happened?

- a) A patient received 60 tablets instead of 30 tablets
- b) A patient received their medication two days late
- c) A patient lost their birth control medication and needed a replacement
- **d) An error happened between two similar generic medication bottles**

Answer: D. An error happened between two similar generic medication bottles. The FDA has the MedWatch program as a way to report adverse events that likely happened because of the labels or packages.

The original name for Prilosec was Losec, but because of its similarity to Lasix, it got changed. It's possible this program would have helped identify the need for the change.

QUESTION O96.

It is a best practice to wipe a counting tray at what interval?

a) After each hour
b) After each shift.
c) After each penicillin or sulfa medication
d) After each use

ANSWER.

It is a best practice to wipe a counting tray at what interval?

   a) After each hour
   b) After each shift.
   c) After each penicillin or sulfa medication
   d) After each use

Answer: D. After each use. This may seem intuitive, but with the number of prescriptions it may seem like a lot of work. However, after every use is the ideal.

QUESTION 097.

While measuring the water to reconstitute a medication, a technician notices the water does not form a straight line, but rather, a bowl in the cylinder. The top of the bowl is at 70 mL, the middle is at 69 mL, and the bottom is at 68 mL. If they use this amount of water, how many mL will they be pouring into the reconstitution?

a) 70 mL
b) 69 mL
c) 68 mL
d) None of these is correct

ANSWER.

While measuring the water to reconstitute a medication, a technician notices the water does not form a straight line, but rather, a bowl in the cylinder. The top of the bowl is at 70 mL, the middle is at 69 mL, and the bottom is at 68 mL. If they use this amount of water, how many mL will they be pouring into the reconstitution?

   a) 70 mL
   b) 69 mL
   c) 68 mL
   d) None of these is correct

Answer: C. 68 mL is the bottom of the meniscus, where the technician should read the line.

QUESTION 098.

What is the value of the FIFO method of inventory control?

a) Places those medicines soonest to expire in the front
b) It provides a means to minimize shelf inventory
c) It provides a way to maximize pharmacy space
d) It is the most economical way of controlling inventory

ANSWER.

What is the value of the FIFO method of inventory control?

a) **Places those medicines soonest to expire in the front**
b) It provides a means to minimize shelf inventory
c) It provides a way to maximize pharmacy space
d) It is the most economical way of controlling inventory

Answer: A. Places those medicines soonest to expire in the front. If you've ever gone into your own fridge and had two things expire at once, you understand the reason for FIFO. However, the extra effort it takes to pull all the old in front of the new sometimes causes this to not happen in practice.

QUESTION 099.

Which administration route is enteral?

a) IM
b) IV
c) SubQ
d) SL

ANSWER.

Which administration route is enteral?

    a) IM
    b) IV
    c) SubQ
    d) SL

Answer: D. SL. It's easiest to explain what enteral and parenteral mean and where they came from. Enteral literally means through the digestive tract and a sublingual dosage form goes under the tongue. However, the word parenteral is actually a shortening of para-enteral. Just as paranormal is outside of normal, para-enteral, or parenteral is outside of the GI tract.

QUESTION 0100.

The parents of a child receiving growth hormone use a fresh needle tip on the medication pen. Where do they properly dispose of this needle?

a) Trash can
b) Recycling container
c) Sharps container
d) Hazardous waste container

ANSWER.

The parents of a child receiving growth hormone use a fresh needle tip on the medication pen. Where do they properly dispose of this needle?

a) Trash can
b) Recycling container
c) **Sharps container**
d) Hazardous waste container

Answer: C. Sharps container. While it may seem easy enough to put a needle in the trash, using the sharps container will make things better for everyone especially when we want to avoid needlesticks.

CHAPTER 10 BODY SYSTEM DRUG LIST WITH SUFFIXES

CHAPTER 1 – GASTROINTESTINAL

I. Peptic Ulcer Disease

Antacids
Calcium Carbonate (Tums)
Magnesium Hydroxide (Milk of Magnesia)

Histamine-2 Receptor Antagonists (H$_2$RAs)
Cimetidine (Tagamet)
Famotidine (Pepcid, Zantac)
Nizatidine (Axid)

Proton Pump Inhibitors (PPIs)
Dexlansoprazole (Dexilant)
Esomeprazole (Nexium)
Omeprazole (Prilosec)
Lansoprazole (Prevacid)
Pantoprazole (Protonix)
Rabeprazole (AcipHex)

II. Diarrhea, IBS, constipation, and emesis

Antidiarrheals
Bismuth Subsalicylate (Pepto-Bismol)
Loperamide (Imodium)
Diphenoxylate / atropine (Lomotil)

Irritable bowel syndrome (IBS)

Dicyclomine (Bentyl)
Hyoscyamine (Anaspaz)

Constipation – Stool softener
Docusate sodium (Colace)

Constipation – Osmotic
Polyethylene glycol (PEG) 3350 (MiraLax)

Constipation – Miscellaneous
Lubiprostone (Amitiza)

Antiemetic – Serotonin 5-HT$_3$ receptor antagonist
Ondansetron (Zofran)

Antiemetic – Phenothiazine
Prochlorperazine (Compazine)
Promethazine (Phenergan)

III. Autoimmune disorders

Ulcerative colitis
Budesonide (Enterocort EC)
Infliximab (Remicade)

CHAPTER 2 – MUSCULOSKELETAL

I. NSAIDs and pain

OTC Analgesics – NSAIDs
Aspirin [ASA] (Ecotrin)
Ibuprofen (Advil, Motrin)
Naproxen (Aleve)

OTC Analgesic – Non-narcotic
Acetaminophen [APAP] (Tylenol)

OTC Migraine – NSAID / Non-narcotic analgesic
ASA/APAP/Caffeine (Excedrin Migraine)

RX Migraine – Narcotic and Non-narcotic analgesic
Butalbital / APAP / Caffeine (Fioricet)

RX Analgesics – NSAIDs
Diclofenac sodium extended release
    (Voltaren XR)
Etodolac (Lodine)
Indomethacin (Indocin)
Meloxicam (Mobic)
Nabumetone (Relafen)

RX Analgesics – NSAIDs – COX-2 inhibitor
Celecoxib (Celebrex)

II. Opioids and narcotics

Opioid analgesics – Schedule II
Morphine (Kadian, MS Contin)
Fentanyl (Duragesic, Sublimaze)
Hydrocodone / Acetaminophen (Vicodin)
Hydrocodone / Chlorpheniramine (Tussionex)

Hydrocodone / Ibuprofen (Vicoprofen)
Methadone (Dolophine)
Oxycodone (OxyIR, Oxycontin)
Oxycodone / Acetaminophen (Percocet)

Opioid analgesics - Schedule III
Acetaminophen w/codeine (Tylenol/codeine)

Mixed-opioid receptor analgesic – Schedule IV
Tramadol (Ultram)
Tramadol / Acetaminophen (Ultracet)

Opioid antagonist
Naloxone (Narcan)
Buprenorphine / Naloxone (Suboxone) [CIII]

III. Headaches and migraine

5-HT$_1$ receptor agonist
Eletriptan (Relpax)
Sumatriptan (Imitrex)

IV. DMARDs and rheumatoid arthritis

Methotrexate (Rheumatrex)
Abatacept (Orencia)
Etanercept (Enbrel)

V. Osteoporosis

Bisphosphonates
Alendronate (Fosamax)
Ibandronate (Boniva)
Risedronate (Actonel)

VI. Selective estrogen receptor modulator (SERM)

Raloxifene (Evista)

VII. Muscle relaxants

Baclofen (Lioresal)
Carisoprodol (Soma)
Cyclobenzaprine (Flexeril)
Diazepam (Valium)
Metaxalone (Skelaxin)
Methocarbamol (Robaxin)
Tizanidine (Zanaflex)

VIII. Gout

Colchicine (Colcrys)

Uric acid reducers
Allopurinol (Zyloprim)
Febuxostat (Uloric)

CHAPTER 3 – RESPIRATORY

I. Antihistamines and decongestants

Antihistamine – 1st-generation
Diphenhydramine (Benadryl)
Hydroxyzine (Atarax)

OTC Antihistamine – 2nd-generation
Cetirizine (Zyrtec)
Loratadine (Claritin)

OTC Antihistamine – 3nd generation
Fexofenadine (Allegra)
Levocetirizine (Xyzal)

OTC Antihistamine – Eye Drops
Olopatadine (Patanol, Pataday)

Antihistamine – Nasal Spray
Azelastine (Astelin)

OTC Antihistamine – 2nd generation /
Decongestant
Loratadine-D (Claritin-D)

BTC/OTC Decongestants
Pseudoephedrine (Sudafed) [BTC]
Phenylephrine (NeoSynephrine) [OTC]
Oxymetazoline (Afrin) [OTC]

II. Allergic rhinitis steroid, antitussives, and mucolytics

Allergic rhinitis steroid
Fluticasone (Flonase)
Mometasone nasal inhaler (Nasonex)

239

Triamcinolone (Nasacort Allergy 24HR)

OTC Antitussive / Mucolytic
Guaifenesin/DM (Mucinex DM, Robitussin DM)

RX Antitussive / Mucolytic
Guaifenesin / Codeine (Cheratussin AC)

RX Antitussive
Benzonatate (Tessalon Perles)

III. Asthma

Oral steroids
Dexamethasone (Decadron)
Methylprednisolone (Medrol)
Prednisone (Deltasone)

Ophthalmic steroid
Loteprednol ophthalmic (Lotemax)

Inhaled steroid / Beta$_2$ receptor agonist
Budesonide / Formoterol (Symbicort)
Fluticasone / Salmeterol (Advair)
Vilanterol / Umeclidinium (Anoro Ellipta)
Fluticasone / Vilanterol / Umeclidinium (Trelegy Ellipta)

Inhaled steroid
Budesonide (Rhinocort, Pulmicort Flexhaler)
Fluticasone (Flonase, Flovent HFA, Flovent Diskus)

Beta$_2$ receptor agonist short acting
Albuterol (ProAir HFA, Proventil)
Levalbuterol (Xopenex HFA)

Beta$_2$ receptor agonist / Anticholinergic

Albuterol / Ipratropium (DuoNeb)
Albuterol / Ipratropium (Combivent)

Anticholinergic
Tiotropium (Spiriva)

Leukotriene receptor antagonist
Montelukast (Singulair)

Anti-IgE antibody
Omalizumab (Xolair)

IV. Anaphylaxis

Epinephrine (EpiPen)

CHAPTER 4 – IMMUNE

I. OTC Antimicrobials

Antibiotic cream
Neomycin / Polymyxin B / Bacitracin (Neosporin)
Mupirocin (Bactroban) [RX]

Antifungal cream
Butenafine (Lotrimin Ultra)
Terbinafine (Lamisil)
Clotrimazole / Betamethasone (Lotrisone) [RX]

Vaccinations [Some RX, some antibacterial]
Influenza vaccine (Fluzone, Flumist)
Varicella (Varivax)
Zoster (Zostavax)

Antiviral OTC
Docosanol (Abreva)

II. Antibiotics that affect the cell wall

Penicillins
Amoxicillin (Amoxil)
Penicillin (Veetids)

Penicillin/Beta-lactamase inhibitor
Amoxicillin / Clavulanate (Augmentin)

Cephalosporins [by generation]
Cephalexin (Keflex) [1st]
Cefuroxime (Ceftin) [2nd]
Cefdinir (Omnicef) [3rd]
Ceftriaxone (Rocephin) [3rd]
Cefepime (Maxipime) [4th]

Ceftaroline (Teflaro) [5th]

Glycopeptide
Vancomycin (Vancocin)

III. Antibiotics – Protein Synthesis Inhibitors (Bacteriostatic)

Tetracyclines
Doxycycline (Doryx)
Minocycline (Minocin)
Tetracycline (Sumycin)

Macrolides
Azithromycin (Zithromax)
Clarithromycin (Biaxin)
Erythromycin (E-Mycin)
Fidaxomicin (Dificid)

Lincosamide
Clindamycin (Cleocin)

Oxazolidinone
Linezolid (Zyvox)

IV. Antibiotics – Protein Synth. Inhibitors (Bactericidal)

Aminoglycosides
Amikacin (Amikin)
Gentamicin (Garamycin)

V. Antibiotics for Urinary Tract Infections (UTIs) and Peptic Ulcer Disease (PUD)

OTC Urinary tract analgesic
Phenazopyridine (Uristat)

Nitrofuran
Nitrofurantoin (Macrobid, Macrodantin)

Dihydrofolate reductase inhibitor
Sulfamethoxazole / Trimethoprim (Bactrim DS)

Fluoroquinolones
Ciprofloxacin (Cipro)
Gatifloxacin ophthalmic (Zymar)
Levofloxacin (Levaquin)
Moxifloxacin (Avelox) / [Ophth. is Vigamox]

Nitroimidazole
Metronidazole (Flagyl)

VI. Anti-tuberculosis agents

Rifampin (Rifadin)
Isoniazid (INH)
Pyrazinamide (PZA)
Ethambutol (Myambutol)

VII. Antifungals

Amphotericin B (Fungizone)
Fluconazole (Diflucan)
Ketoconazole (Nizoral)
Nystatin (Mycostatin)

VIII. Antivirals – Non-HIV

Influenza A and B
Oseltamivir (Tamiflu)
Zanamivir (Relenza)

Herpes simplex virus & Varicella-Zoster Virus
HSV/VSV

Acyclovir (Zovirax)
Valacyclovir (Valtrex)

Respiratory Syncytial Virus RSV
156. Palivizumab (Synagis)

Hepatitis
Entecavir (Baraclude)
Hepatitis A (Havrix)
Hepatitis B (Recombivax HB)

HPV
Human papillomavirus (Gardasil)

IX. Antivirals – HIV

Fusion Inhibitor
Enfuvirtide (Fuzeon) (T-20)

CCR5 Antagonist
Maraviroc (Selzentry) (MVC)
Non-nucleoside reverse transcriptase inhibitors
(NNRTI) with two nucleoside / nucleotide reverse
transcriptase inhibitors (NRTIs)
Efavirenz (Sustiva) [NNRTI]
Emtricitabine / Tenofovir (Truvada) [NRTIs]
Efavirenz / Emtricitabine / Tenofovir (Atripla)
[NNRTI / NRTIs] (EFV / FTC / TDF)

Integrase Strand Transfer Inhibitor
Raltegravir (Isentress) (RAL)

Protease Inhibitor
Atazanavir (Reyataz) (ATV)
Darunavir (Prezista) (DRV)

X. Miscellaneous

Albendazole (Albenza) [Anthelmintic]
Hydroxychloroquine (Plaquenil) [Antimalarial]
Nitazoxanide (Alinia) [Antiprotozoal]

CHAPTER 5 – NEURO

I. OTC Local anesthetics and antivertigo

Local anesthetics
Benzocaine (Anbesol) [Ester type]
Lidocaine (Solarcaine) [Amide type]

Antivertigo
Meclizine (Dramamine, Antivert [RX])

II. Sedative-hypnotics (Sleeping pills)

OTC Non-narcotic analgesic / Sedative-hypnotic
Acetaminophen PM (Tylenol PM)

Benzodiazepine-like
Eszopiclone (Lunesta)
Zolpidem (Ambien)

Melatonin receptor agonist
Ramelteon (Rozerem)

Miscellaneous
Trazodone (Desyrel)

III. Antidepressants

Miscellaneous / SSRI
Vilazodone (Viibryd)

Selective serotonin reuptake inhibitors (SSRIs)
Citalopram (Celexa)
Escitalopram (Lexapro)
Sertraline (Zoloft)
Fluoxetine (Prozac, Sarafem)

Paroxetine (Paxil, Paxil CR)

Serotonin-Norepinephrine reuptake inhibitors
(SNRIs)
Duloxetine (Cymbalta)
Desvenlafaxine (Pristiq)
Venlafaxine (Effexor)

Tricyclic antidepressants (TCAs)
Amitriptyline (Elavil)
Doxepin (Sinequan)
Nortriptyline (Pamelor)

Tetracycylic antidepressant (TeCA) Noradrenergic
and specific serotonergic antidepressants (NaSSAs)
Mirtazapine (Remeron)

Monoamine oxidase inhibitor (MAOI)
Isocarboxazid (Marplan)

IV. Smoking Cessation

Bupropion (Wellbutrin, Zyban)
Varenicline (Chantix)

V. Barbiturates

196. Phenobarbital (Luminal)

VI. Benzodiazepines

Clonazepam (Klonopin)
Alprazolam (Xanax)
Lorazepam (Ativan)
Midazolam (Versed)
Temazepam (Restoril)

VII. Non-benzodiazepine / non-barbiturate

Buspirone (Buspar)

VIII. ADHD medications

Stimulant – Schedule II
Amphetamine/Dextroamphetamine (Adderall)
Dexmethylphenidate (Focalin)
Lisdexamfetamine (Vyvanse)
Methylphenidate (Concerta)

Non-stimulant – non-scheduled
Atomoxetine (Strattera)

IX. Bipolar Disorder

Simple salt
Lithium (Lithobid)

XI. Schizophrenia

First generation antipsychotic (FGA) (low potency)
Chlorpromazine (Thorazine)

First generation antipsychotic (FGA) (high potency)
Haloperidol (Haldol)

Second-generation antipsychotic (SGA)
Aripiprazole (Abilify)
Clozapine (Clozaril)
Olanzapine (Zyprexa)
Risperidone (Risperdal)
Quetiapine (Seroquel)
Ziprasidone (Geodon)

XII. Antiepileptics

Traditional antiepileptics
Carbamazepine (Tegretol)
Divalproex (Depakote)
Phenytoin (Dilantin)

Newer antiepileptics
Gabapentin (Neurontin)
Lamotrigine (Lamictal)
Levetiracetam (Keppra)
Oxcarbazepine (Trileptal)
Pregabalin (Lyrica)
Topiramate (Topamax)

XIII. Parkinson's, Alzheimer's, Motion sickness

Parkinson's
Benztropine mesylate (Cogentin)
Levodopa / Carbidopa (Sinemet)
Selegiline (Eldepryl)
Pramipexole (Mirapex ER)
Ropinirole (Requip, Requip XL)

Alzheimer's
Donepezil (Aricept)
Memantine (Namenda)

Motion sickness
Scopolamine (Transderm-Scop)

CHAPTER 6 – CARDIO

I. OTC Antihyperlipidemics and antiplatelet

Antihyperlipidemics
Omega-3-acid ethyl esters (Lovaza)

Niacin (Niaspan ER)

<u>Antiplatelet</u>
Aspirin (Ecotrin)

II. Diuretics

<u>Osmotic</u>
Mannitol (Osmitrol)

<u>Loop</u>
Furosemide (Lasix)

<u>Thiazide</u>
Hydrochlorothiazide (Microzide)

<u>Potassium sparing and thiazide</u>
Triamterene/Hydrochlorothiazide (Dyazide)

<u>Potassium sparing</u>
Spironolactone (Aldactone)

<u>Electrolyte replenishment</u>
Potassium chloride (K-DUR)

III. Understanding the Alphas and Betas

<u>Alpha-1 antagonist</u>
Doxazosin (Cardura)
Terazosin (Hytrin)

<u>Alpha-2 agonist</u>
Clonidine (Catapres)

<u>Beta-blocker – 1st-generation – non-beta selective</u>
Propranolol (Inderal)

Beta-blockers – 2nd-generation – beta selective
Aten<u>olol</u> (Tenormin)
Aten<u>olol</u> / Chlorthalidone (Tenoretic)
Bisop<u>rolol</u> / Hydroch<u>lorothiazide</u> (Ziac)
Metop<u>rolol</u> succinate (Toprol-XL)
Metop<u>rolol</u> tartrate (Lopressor)

Beta-blocker – 3rd-generation – non-beta selective
vasodilating
Carve<u>dilol</u> (Coreg)
Labe<u>talol</u> (Normodyne)
Nebiv<u>olol</u> (Bystolic)

IV. Renin-angiotensin-aldosterone system (RAAS)

ACE Inhibitors (ACEIs)
Benaze<u>pril</u> / HCTZ (Lotensin HCT)
Enala<u>pril</u> (Vasotec)
Fosinopril (Monopril)
Quina<u>pril</u> (Accupril)
Lisino<u>pril</u> (Zestril)
Lisino<u>pril</u> / Hydrochlo<u>rothiazide</u> (Zestoretic)
Rami<u>pril</u> (Altace)

Angiotensin II receptor blockers (ARBs)
Cande<u>sartan</u> (Atacand)
Irbe<u>sartan</u> (Avapro)
Irbe<u>sartan</u> / Hydrochlo<u>rothiazide</u> (Avalide)
Lo<u>sartan</u> (Cozaar)
Lo<u>sartan</u> / Hydrochlorothiazide (Hyzaar)
Olme<u>sartan</u> (Benicar)
Olme<u>sartan</u> / HCTZ (Benicar HCT)
Telmi<u>sartan</u> / HCTZ (Micardis HCT)
Val<u>sartan</u> (Diovan)
Val<u>sartan</u> / HCTZ (Diovan HCT)

Angiotensin Receptor Neprilysin Inhibitor (ARNI)
Valsartan / Sacubitril (Entresto)

V. Calcium channel blockers (CCBs)

Non-dihydropyridines
Diltiazem (Cardizem)
Verapamil (Calan)

Dihydropyridines
Amlodipine (Norvasc)
Amlodipine / Atorvastatin (Caduet)
Amlodipine / Benazepril (Lotrel)
Amlodipine / Valsartan (Exforge)
Felodipine (Plendil)
Nifedipine (Procardia)

VI. Vasodilators

Hydralazine (Apresoline)
Isosorbide mononitrate (Imdur)
Nitroglycerin (Nitrostat)

VII. Anti-anginal

Ranolazine (Ranexa)

VIII. Antihyperlipidemics

HMG-CoA reductase inhibitors
Atorvastatin (Lipitor)
Lovastatin (Mevacor)
Pravastatin (Pravachol)
Rosuvastatin (Crestor)
Simvastatin (Zocor)

Fibric acid derivatives

Feno<u>fibrate</u> (Tricor)
Gem<u>fibr</u>ozil (Lopid)

<u>Bile acid sequestrant</u>
Colesevelam (Welchol)

<u>Cholesterol absorption blocker</u>
Eze<u>timibe</u> (Zetia)
Eze<u>timibe</u> / Sim<u>vastatin</u> (Vytorin)

IX. Anticoagulants and antiplatelets

<u>Anticoagulants</u>
Enoxa<u>parin</u> (Lovenox)
He<u>parin</u>
War<u>farin</u> (Coumadin)
Dabi<u>gatran</u> (Pradaxa)
Rivaro<u>xaban</u> (Xarelto)
Apixaban (Eliquis)

<u>Antiplatelet</u>
Aspirin / Dipyridamole (Aggrenox)
Clopido<u>grel</u> (Plavix)
Prasu<u>grel</u> (Effient)
Tica<u>grel</u>or (Brilinta)

X. Cardiac glycoside and Anticholinergic

<u>Cardiac glycoside</u>
Digoxin (Lanoxin)

<u>Anticholinergic</u>
A<u>tro</u>pine (AtroPen)

XI. Antidysrhythmic
Amiodarone (Cordarone)

Chapter 10 Full Drug List

CHAPTER 7 – ENDOCRINE / MISC.

I. OTC Insulin and emergency contraception

> 306. Regular Insulin (Humulin R)
> 307. NPH Insulin (Humulin N)
> 308. Levonorgestrel (Plan B One-Step)

II. Diabetes and insulin

> Biguanides
> Metformin (Glucophage)
> Metformin / Glyburide (Glucovance)
>
> DPP-4 Inhibitors (Gliptins)
> Linagliptin (Tradjenta)
> Saxagliptin (Onglyza)
> Sitagliptin (Januvia)
>
> Meglitinides (Glinides)
> Repaglinide (Prandin)
>
> Sulfonylureas – 2nd-generation
> Glyburide (DiaBeta)
> Glimepiride (Amaryl)
> Glipizide (Glucotrol)
>
> Thiazolidinediones (Glitazones)
> Pioglitazone (Actos)
> Rosiglitazone (Avandia)
>
> Incretin mimetics
> Exenatide (Byetta)
> Liraglutide (Victoza)
>
> Hypoglycemia

Glucagon (GlucaGen)

<u>RX Insulin</u>
Insulin aspart (Novolog)
Insulin lispro (Humalog)
Insulin detemir (Levemir)
Insulin glargine (Lantus, Toujeo)

III. Thyroid hormones

<u>Hypothyroidism</u>
Levothyroxine (Synthroid)

<u>Hyperthyroidism</u>
Propylthiouracil (PTU)

IV. Hormones and contraception

<u>Low testosterone</u>
Testosterone (AndroGel)

<u>Estrogens and / or Progestins</u>
Estradiol (Estrace, Estraderm)
Conjugated estrogens (Premarin)
Conjugated estrogens / Medroxyprogesterone
        (Prempro, Premphase)
Progesterone (Prometrium)
Medroxyprogesterone (Provera)

<u>Combined oral contraceptive pill (COCP)</u>
Ethinyl estradiol / norethindrone / Fe
(Loestrin 24 Fe)
Ethinyl estradiol / norgestimate (Tri-Sprintec)

<u>Patch</u>
Ethinyl estradiol / norelgestromin (OrthoEvra)

Ring
Ethinyl estradiol / etonogestrel (NuvaRing)

V. Overactive bladder, urinary retention, erectile dysfunction (ED), benign prostatic hyperplasia (BPH)

Overactive bladder
Oxybutynin (Ditropan)
Darifenacin (Enablex)
Solifenacin (VESIcare)
Tolterodine (Detrol)

Urinary retention
Bethanechol (Urecholine)

Erectile dysfunction - PDE-5 inhibitors
Sildenafil (Viagra)
Vardenafil (Levitra)
Tadalafil (Cialis)

BPH – Alpha-blocker
Alfuzosin (Uroxatral)
Tamsulosin (Flomax)

BPH – 5-alpha-reducase inhibitor
Dutasteride (Avodart)
Finasteride (Proscar, Propecia)

the ground, so the brand **Levitra** hints at the rising erection.

CHAPTER 11 THE OTC SCAVENGER HUNT

I learned drug names by working in a pharmacy. I recommend you start learning them with this lab activity. Medications you have held will be easier to memorize. If you are in the car driving and listening to the audio version of this book, obviously, just keep going, but I encourage you to try this activity when you have a chance.

Picture finding the drugs in an alphabetical list. It's not very conducive to memorization.

Acetaminophen
Acetaminophen PM
ASA/APAP/Caffeine
Aspirin (Low Dose)
Aspirin (Regular)
Benzocaine
Bismuth subsalicylate
Butenafine
Calcium carbonate
Cetirizine
Diphenhydramine
Docosanol
Docusate sodium
Esomeprazole

Famotidine
Guaifenesin/DM
Ibuprofen
Influenza vaccine
NPH insulin
Regular insulin
Levonorgestrel
Lidocaine
Loperamide
Loratadine
Loratadine-D
Magnesium hydroxide
Meclizine
Naproxen

Neomycin /
   Polymyxin B /
   Bacitracin
Niacin
Omega-3 E.E.
Omeprazole
Oxymetazoline
Phenylephrine
Polyethylene gly.
Pseudoephedrine
Nizatidine
Triamcinolone

Now picture (or actually find) this list sorted by pathophysio-logic class. This is how pharmacies sort over-the-counter (OTC) drugs for placement on drug store shelves.

Gastrointestinal

Calcium carbonate	Esomeprazole	Docusate sodium
Magnesium hydroxide	Omeprazole	Polyethylene gly.

Memorizing Pharmacology

| Famotidine | Bismuth subsalicylate |
| Nizatidine | Loperamide |

Musculoskeletal

Aspirin (Regular)	Acetaminophen
Ibuprofen	Acetaminophen / Aspirin / Caffeine
Naproxen	

Respiratory

Diphenhydramine	Loratadine-D	Oxymetazoline
Cetirizine	Pseudoephedrine	Triamcinolone
Loratadine	Phenylephrine	Guaifenesin / DM

Immune

Neomycin /	Butenafine
Polymyxin B /	Docosanol
Bacitracin	Influenza vaccine

Neuro

| Benzocaine | Meclizine | Acetaminophen PM |
| Lidocaine | | |

Cardio

| Omega-3-Fatty E.E. | Niacin | Aspirin (Low Dose) |

Endocrine

| Regular insulin | NPH insulin | Levonorgestrel |

You will find the second list often grouped together in the pharmacy aisles. The same is true in your brain. It remembers drugs in related groups, not in strict alphabetical order, a better way to remember them.

ALPHABETICAL LIST OF STEMS

ac	anti-inflammatory agents (<u>ac</u>etic <u>ac</u>id derivatives)
adol	analgesics (mixed opiate receptor agonists/antagonists)
afil	phosphodiesterase type 5 (PDE5) inhibitors
alol	combined alpha and beta blockers
amivir	neuraminidase inhibitors
astine	antihistaminics (histamine-H_1 receptor antagonists)
atadine	tricyclic histaminic-H_1 receptor antagonists, lor<u>ata-dine</u> derivatives (formerly -tadine)
azepam	antianxiety agents (di<u>azepam</u> type)
azolam	(WHO stem) diazepam derivatives
azosin	antihypertensives (pr<u>azosin</u> type)
barb	<u>barb</u>ituric acid derivatives
bendazole	anthelmintics (ti<u>bendazole</u> type)
caine	local anesthetics
cavir	carbocyclic nucleosides
cef	cephalosporins
citabine	nucleoside antiviral / antineoplastic agents, cytarabine or azarabine derivatives
cillin	peni<u>cillin</u>s
clone	hypnotics/tranquilizers (zopi<u>clone</u> type)
conazole	systemic antifungals (mi<u>conazole</u> type)
coxib	cyclooxygenase-2 inhibitors
cycline	antibiotics (tetra<u>cycline</u> derivatives)
cyclovir	antivirals (a<u>cyclovir</u> type)
dil	vaso<u>dil</u>ators (undefined group)
dipine	phenylpyridine vasodilators (nife<u>dipine</u> type)
dopa	<u>dopa</u>mine receptor agonists
dralazine	antihypertensives (hyd<u>ralazine</u>-phthalazines)
drine	sympathomimetics

261

dronate	calcium metabolism regulators
estr	<u>estr</u>ogens
farin	war<u>farin</u> analogs
faxine	antianxiety, antidepressant inhibitor of norepinephrine and dopamine re-uptake
fenacin	muscarinic receptor antagonists
fetamine	am<u>fetamine</u> derivatives
fibrate	antihyperlipidemics (clo<u>fibrate</u> type)
floxacin	fluoroquinolone (not on Stem List)
formin	hypoglycemics (phen<u>formin</u> type)
gab	<u>gab</u>amimetics
gatran	thrombin inhibitors (ar<u>gatr</u>o<u>ban</u> type)
gest	pro<u>gest</u>ins
giline	Monoamine oxidase (MAO) inhibitors, type B
gli (was gly)	antihyperglycemics
glinide	antidiabetic, sodium glucose co-transporter 2 (SGLT2) inhibitors, not phlorozin derivatives
gliptin	dipeptidyl aminopeptidase-IV inhibitors
glitazone	peroxisome proliferator activating receptor (PPAR) agonists (thiazolidene derivatives)
glutide	<u>glu</u>cagon-like pep<u>tide</u> (GLP) analogs
gly	antihyper<u>gly</u>cemics
grel	platelet aggregation inhibitors, primarily platelet P2Y12 receptor antagonists
icam	anti-inflammatory agents (isox<u>icam</u> type)
ifene	antiestrogens of the clom<u>ifene</u> and tamox<u>ifen</u> groups
imibe	antihyperlipidaemics, acyl CoA: cholesterol acyltransferase (ACAT) inhibitors
iodarone	indicates high iodine content antiarrhythmic
kacin	antibiotics obtained from *Streptomyces kanamyceticus* (related to kanamy<u>cin</u>)

liximab	monoclonal antibodies
lizumab	monoclonal antibodies
lukast	leukotriene receptor antagonists
mantine	antivirals/antiparkinsonians (adamantane derivatives)
melteon	selective melatonin receptor agonist
methacin	anti-inflammatory agents (indo<u>methacin</u> type)
micin	antibiotics (*Micromonospora* strains)
mycin	antibiotics (*Streptomyces* strain)
nal	narcotic agonists/antagonists (normorphine type)
navir	HIV protease inhibitors (saqui<u>navir</u> type)
nercept	tumor necrosis factor receptors
nicline	<u>ni</u>cotinic acetylcho<u>line</u> receptor partial agonists/agonists
nidazole	antiprotozoal substances (metro<u>nidazole</u> type)
nifur	5-<u>nitrofur</u>an derivatives
nitro	(WHO stem) NO_2 derivatives
olol	beta-blockers (propran<u>olol</u> type)
orphan	narcotic antagonists/agonists (m<u>orphan</u> derivatives)
oxacin	antibacterials (quinolone derivatives)
oxanide	antiparasitics (salicylanilide derivatives)
oxetine	antidepressants (flu<u>oxetine</u> type)
pamil	coronary vasodilators (vera<u>pamil</u> type)
parin	he<u>parin</u> derivatives and low molecular weight (or depolymerized) heparins
peg	<u>PEG</u>ylated compounds, covalent attachment of macrogol (pol<u>ye</u>thylene <u>g</u>lycol) polymer
peridol	antipsychotics (halo<u>peridol</u> type)
peridone	antipsychotics (ris<u>peridone</u> type)
pezil	acetylcholinesterase inhibitors used in the treatment of Alzheimer's disease

pidem	hypnotics/sedatives (zol<u>pidem</u> type)
pin(e)	tricyclic compounds
piprazole	(WHO stem) psychotropics, phenylpiperazine derivatives (future use is discouraged due to conflict with stem -prazole)
prazole	antiulcer agents (benzimidazole derivatives)
pred	<u>pred</u>nisone and <u>pred</u>nisolone derivatives
pril	antihypertensives (ACE inhibitors)
prim	antibacterials (trimetho<u>prim</u> type)
profen	anti-inflammatory/analgesic agents (ibu<u>profen</u> type)
prost	<u>prost</u>aglandins
racetam	nootropic agents (learning, cognitive enhancers), pi<u>racetam</u> type
rifa	antibiotics (<u>rifa</u>mycin derivatives)
sal	anti-inflammatory agents (<u>sal</u>icylic acid derivatives)
sartan	angiotensin II receptor antagonists
semide	diuretics (furo<u>semide</u> type)
setron	serotonin 5-HT$_3$ receptor antagonists
sidone	antipsychotic with binding activity on serotonin (5-HT2A) and dopamine (D2) receptors
spirone	anxiolytics (bu<u>spirone</u> type)
ster	<u>ster</u>oids (androgens, anabolics)
steride	testosterone reductase inhibitors
sulfa	antimicrobials (<u>sulfa</u>mides derivatives)
tacept	<u>T-cept</u>ors
tegravir	in<u>tegra</u>se inhibitors
terol	bronchodilators (phenethylamine derivatives)
thiazide	diuretics (<u>thiazide</u> derivatives)
thromycin	macrolide (not on Stem List)
tiapine	antipsychotics (dibenzo<u>thiaze</u>pine derivatives)
tiazem	calcium channel blockers (dil<u>tiazem</u> type)

tide	pep<u>tide</u>s
tidine	H₂-receptor antagonists (cime<u>tidine</u> type)
toin	antiepileptics (hydan<u>toin</u> derivatives)
traline	selective serotonin reuptake inhibitors (SSRI)
trexate	antimetabolites (folic acid derivatives)
tril	endopeptidase inhibitors (e.g. neprilysin)
triptan	antimigraine agents (5-HT₁ receptor agonists); suma<u>triptan</u> derivatives
triptyline	antidepressants (dibenzol[a.d.]cycloheptane derivatives)
trop(ium)	<u>atrop</u>ine derivative, (quaternary ammonium salt)
trop(ine)	<u>atrop</u>ine derivatives; Subgroups: tertiary amines (e.g., benztropine)
uracil	<u>uracil</u> derivatives used as thyroid antagonists and as antineoplastics
vastatin	antihyperlipidemics (HMG-CoA inhibitors)
vir	anti<u>vir</u>als
virenz	non-nucleoside reverse transcriptase inhibitors; benzoxazinone derivatives
viroc	CC chemokine receptor type 5 (CCR5) antagonists
vudine	antineoplastics; antivirals (zido<u>vudine</u> group) (exception: edoxudine)
xaban	antithrombotics, blood coagulation factor XA inhibitors
xostat	xanthine oxidase/dehydrogenase inhibitors
zolid	oxa<u>zolid</u>inone antibacterials

LIST OF STEMS BY PHYSIOLOGIC CLASS

Chapter 1: Gastrointestinal

liximab	monoclonal antibodies
peg	PEGylated compounds, covalent attachment of macrogol (polyethylene glycol) polymer
prazole	antiulcer agents (benzimidazole derivatives)
prost	prostaglandins
sal	anti-inflammatory agents (salicylic acid derivatives)
setron	serotonin 5-HT$_3$ receptor antagonists
tidine	H$_2$-receptor antagonists (cimetidine type)

Chapter 2: Musculoskeletal

ac	anti-inflammatory agents (acetic acid derivatives)
adol	analgesics (mixed opiate receptor agonists/antagonists)
coxib	cyclooxygenase-2 inhibitors
dronate	calcium metabolism regulators
icam	anti-inflammatory agents (isoxicam type)
ifene	antiestrogens of the clomifene and tamoxifen groups
liximab	monoclonal antibodies
methacin	anti-inflammatory agents (indomethacin type)
nal	narcotic agonists/antagonists (normorphine type)
nercept	tumor necrosis factor receptors
profen	anti-inflammatory/analgesic agents (ibuprofen type)
tacept	T-cell receptors
trexate	antimetabolites (folic acid derivatives)
triptan	antimigraine agents (5-HT$_1$ receptor agonists); sumatriptan derivatives
xostat	xanthine oxidase/dehydrogenase inhibitors

APPENDIX

Chapter 3: Respiratory

atadine	tricyclic histaminic-H$_1$ receptor antagonists, loratadine derivatives (formerly -tadine)
astine	antihistaminics (histamine-H$_1$ receptor antagonists)
drine	sympathomimetics
lizumab	monoclonal antibodies
lukast	leukotriene receptor antagonists
orphan	narcotic antagonists/agonists (morphinan derivatives)
pred	prednisone and prednisolone derivatives
terol	bronchodilators (phenethylamine derivatives)
trop(ium)	atropine derivative (quaternary ammonium salt)

Chapter 4: Immune

amivir	neuraminidase inhibitors
bendazole	anthelmintics (tibendazole type)
cavir	carbocyclic nucleosides
cef	cephalosporins
cillin	penicillins
citabine	nucleoside antiviral / antineoplastic agents, cytarabine or azarabine derivatives
conazole	systemic antifungals (miconazole type)
cycline	antibiotics (tetracycline derivatives)
cyclovir	antivirals (acyclovir type)
floxacin	fluoroquinolone (not on Stem List)
kacin	antibiotics obtained from *Streptomyces kanamyceticus* (related to kanamycin)
lizumab	monoclonal antibodies
micin	antibiotics (*Micromonospora* strains)
mycin	antibiotics (*Streptomyces* strain)
navir	HIV protease inhibitors (saquinavir type)
nidazole	antiprotozoal substances (metronidazole type)
nifur	5-nitrofuran derivatives
oxacin	antibacterials (quinolone derivatives)
oxanide	antiparasitics (salicylanilide derivatives)
prim	antibacterials (trimethoprim type)

rifa	antibiotics (<u>rifa</u>mycin derivatives)
sulfa	antimicrobials (<u>sulfona</u>mides derivatives)
tegravir	in<u>tegra</u>se inhibitors
thromycin	macrolide (not on Stem List)
vir	anti<u>vir</u>als
virenz	non-nucleoside reverse transcriptase inhibitors; benzoxazinone derivatives
viroc	CC chemokine receptor type 5 (CCR5) antagonists
vudine	antineoplastics; antivirals (zido<u>vudine</u> group) (exception: edoxudine)
zolid	oxa<u>zolid</u>inone antibacterials

Chapter 5: Neuro

azepam	antianxiety agents (di<u>azepam</u> type)
azolam	(WHO stem) diazepam derivatives
caine	local anesthetics
clone	hypnotics/tranquilizers (zopi<u>clone</u> type)
dopa	<u>dopa</u>mine receptor agonists
faxine	antianxiety, antidepressant inhibitor of norepinephrine and dopamine re-uptake
gab	<u>gab</u>amimetics
giline	Monoamine oxidase (MAO) inhibitors, type B
melteon	selective melatonin receptor agonist
oxetine	antidepressants (flu<u>oxetine</u> type)
peridol	antipsychotics (halo<u>peridol</u> type)
peridone	antipsychotics (ris<u>peridone</u> type)
pezil	acetylcholinesterase inhibitors used in the treatment of Alzheimer's disease
pidem	hypnotics/sedatives (zol<u>pidem</u> type)
pin(e)	tricyclic compounds
tiapine	antipsychotics (dibenzothiazepine derivatives)
toin	antiepileptics (hydan<u>toin</u> derivatives)
traline	selective serotonin reuptake inhibitors (SSRI)
triptyline	antidepressants (dibenzol[a,d] cycloheptane derivatives)
nicline	<u>ni</u>cotinic acetylcho<u>line</u> receptor partial agonists/agonists

APPENDIX

barb	barbituric acid derivatives
spirone	anxiolytics (buspirone type)
fetamine	amfetamine derivatives
piprazole	(WHO stem) psychotropics, phenylpiperazine derivatives (future use is discouraged due to conflict with stem -prazole)
racetam	nootropic agents (learning, cognitive enhancers), piracetam type
sidone	antipsychotic with binding activity on serotonin (5-HT2A) and dopamine (D2) receptors
tropine	atropine derivatives; Subgroups: tertiary amines (e.g., benztropine)
mantine	antivirals/antiparkinsonians (adamantane derivatives)

Chapter 6: Cardio

alol	combined alpha and beta blockers
azosin	antihypertensives (prazosin type)
dil	vasodilators (undefined group)
dipine	phenylpyridine vasodilators (nifedipine type)
dralazine	antihypertensives (hydrazine-phthalazines)
farin	warfarin analogs
fibrate	antihyperlipidemics (clofibrate type)
gatran	thrombin inhibitors (argatroban type)
grel	platelet aggregation inhibitors, primarily platelet P2Y12 receptor antagonists
imibe	antihyperlipidaemics, acyl CoA: cholesterol acyltransferase (ACAT) inhibitors
iodarone	indicates high iodine content antiarrhythmic
nitro	(WHO stem) NO_2 derivatives
olol	beta-blockers (propranolol type)
pamil	coronary vasodilators (verapamil type)
parin	heparin derivatives and low molecular weight (or depolymerized) heparins
pril	antihypertensives (ACE inhibitors)
sartan	angiotensin II receptor antagonists
semide	diuretics (furosemide type)
thiazide	diuretics (thiazide derivatives)

tiazem	calcium channel blockers (dil<u>tiazem</u> type)
tril	endopeptidase inhibitors (e.g. neprilysin)
trop(ine)	atropine derivatives; Subgroups: tertiary amines (e.g., benz<u>tropine</u>)
vastatin	antihyperlipidemics (HMG-CoA inhibitors)
xaban	antithrombotics, blood coagulation factor XA inhibitors

Chapter 7: Endocrine / Misc.

afil	phosphodiesterase type 5 (PDE5) inhibitors
estr	<u>estr</u>ogens
fenacin	muscarinic receptor antagonists
formin	hypoglycemics (phen<u>formin</u> type)
gest	pro<u>gest</u>ins
gli (was gly)	antihyperglycemics
glinide	antidiabetic, sodium glucose co-transporter 2 (SGLT2) inhibitors, not phlorozin derivatives
gliptin	dipeptidyl aminopeptidase-IV inhibitors
glitazone	peroxisome proliferator activating receptor (PPAR) agonists (thiazolidene derivatives)
glutide	<u>glu</u>cagon-like pep<u>tide</u> (GLP) analogs
gly	antihyper<u>gly</u>cemics
ster	<u>ster</u>oids (androgens, anabolics)
steride	testosterone reductase inhibitors
tide	pep<u>tide</u>s
uracil	<u>uracil</u> derivatives used as thyroid antagonists and as antineoplastics

Generic and Brand Name Index

Generic and Brand Name Index

Generic and Brand Name Index

Generic and Brand Name Index

Generic and Brand Name Index

Made in the USA
Las Vegas, NV
15 January 2023

65688644R00166